Riddle of the Future

Also by Andrew MacKenzie

THE UNEXPLAINED

FRONTIERS OF THE UNKNOWN

APPARITIONS AND GHOSTS

A GALLERY OF GHOSTS

Riddle of the Future

a modern study of precognition

Andrew MacKenzie

with a preface by Robert H. Thouless, Ph.D., Sc.D.

Taplinger Publishing Company / New York

First published in the United States in 1975 by
TAPLINGER PUBLISHING CO., INC.
New York, New York

Library of Congress Catalog Card Nunber: 75–8199

ISBN 0–8008–6795–5

Contents

This morning as I was shaving I thought of a friend of mine who lives in Madrid and whom I haven't seen for fifteen years. Looking at my own image in the mirror, I asked myself whether, after so long, we would recognize each other immediately if we met by accident in the street. I pictured to myself our meeting in Madrid and I began to imagine his feelings. He is a friend to whom I am deeply attached, but I hear from him only once or twice a year and he does not occupy a constant place in my thoughts. After I had shaved, I went down to my letterbox and there found a ten-page letter from him.

Such 'coincidences' are not uncommon and everyone is more or less familiar with them. They offer us an insight into how approximate and arbitrary is our normal reading of time. Calendars and clocks are our inadequate inventions. The structure of our minds is such that the true nature of time usually escapes us. Yet we know there is a mystery. Like a never-seen object in the dark, we can feel our way over some of its surfaces. But we have not identified it.

John Berger, *G.*

Experience is the *only* evidence

R. D. Laing, *The Politics of Experience.*

Preface

Much of the foretelling of the future is a perfectly normal activity, posing no riddles. Our newspapers, no less than the manuals of fortune-tellers, are largely concerned with forecasts of future events – of tomorrow's weather, of how much the cost of living is going to rise, of when an eclipse of the moon will take place, and so on. Many of these were also of practical concern to our remote ancestors and they had other techniques of foretelling the future which included examination of the entrails of sacrificed animals, observation of the flight of birds, and the interpretation of dreams. It is perhaps because we have many more reliable normal means of foretelling the future, that we are less concerned than were our ancestors with such paranormal means of doing it. Yet there remains evidence that the future may occasionally be foretold by means that are not normal, that are not rational inferences from what is happening now.

In the present book, Mr MacKenzie has made a careful collection of many spontaneous cases of apparent paranormal foretelling of the future. These form an impressive body of evidence that such paranormal precognition does at times occur, however unwilling the majority of people may be to believe in it. Such a collection of spontaneous cases as is presented here creates a strong case for the reality of paranormal precognition; it might not, in itself, be enough to create conviction in the minds of those inclined to scepticism. To my mind, the matter needs clinching by experimental evidence. If it is claimed that some people can receive a warning of disaster before this happens, it is natural to ask whether anyone can foretell, before it is shuffled and cut, the future order of a pack of cards. Experimental work carried out at the Rhine laboratory and elsewhere shows that they can do so to an extent that goes beyond the possibility of explanation by chance. Knowledge of this fact should make one more ready to accept the possibility of some people foreseeing the disasters of Aberfan and of the *Titanic* without any possibility of inferring by normal means that they were going to happen. The twin supports of observation of spontaneous cases and of experimental confirmation render the total case for the reality of paranormal precognition very strong indeed.

The first question to be answered about paranormal precognition is whether or not it occurs. If it occurs, it must be accepted as a fact whether or not we can explain how it could happen. If its occurrence contradicts our expectations as to what should happen, we must revise our expectations. It looks as if the revision of expectations that is necessary to accommodate precognition must involve a change in our common-sense way of thinking about time; we should be prepared for the necessity of such a change in our thinking. There is nothing sacred about 'common sense'; it may only be the name for our firmly established habits of thought.

This is, no doubt, the difficulty that many people find in accepting the reality of paranormal precognition. It is not that the evidence for it is weak, but that people find it particularly hard to conceive of precognition being a reality. It is arguable that this attitude is not altogether reasonable and that there is a tendency to exaggerate the inconceivability of precognition as compared with other paranormal phenomena, e.g. telepathy. People may also be wrong in too easily accepting conceivability as a criterion of what is the case: that we find something inconceivable may only indicate an unfortunate limitation in our powers of conceiving.

However this may be, there is no doubt that many people do find it difficult to believe in the possibility of paranormal precognition and that this difficulty often leads them to reject the very strong evidence that there is for its reality. The kernel of this difficulty is pointed out by Mr MacKenzie: that the non-inferential foreseeing of a future event seems to imply that this event has produced an effect before it has itself taken place, which seems to contradict our idea of the nature of causation and time.

Various ways have been proposed of getting over this difficulty. It was suggested by Dunne that the future event has, in some sense, already taken place, not in time as we know it, but in the time in which this time unrolls itself. Perhaps it will be remembered as a principal contribution of Dunne to this subject, that he realized that a rethinking of the nature of time was a necessary preliminary to understanding how paranormal precognition could take place. I agree with Mr MacKenzie, however, that Dunne's own attempt at this rethinking will not do. Apart from the fact that the idea of a time in which time unrolls itself entails an infinite series of times in which the previous time unrolls itself, one may question whether the idea of a time in which time unrolls itself is not merely a muddle based on the misuse of language. The problem remains, however: if we are to understand precognition, it seems that we must reconsider our idea of time. How we are to think about time remains an open question. The answer is not likely to be found without many attempts that will have to be afterwards discarded.

Of the ideas about precognition and time currently floating about, I find myself especially attracted by the suggestions made by Dr Targ at the 1972 convention of the Parapsychological Association at Edinburgh.[1] He invites us to suppose that the single direction of time with information always flowing in the direction from the past to the future may not be a logical necessity but a firmly based habit of thought. Perhaps an event producing strong effects after its occurrence may also produce a weak effect earlier in time. A paranormal precognition might be such a weak effect, earlier in time than the event producing it. If we have the experience of waking up just before the alarm clock goes off, this might be an example of an event with strong after-effects producing a weak effect earlier in time.

It is unlikely that anyone has the answer yet to these puzzles about precognition. More has to be found out and more thinking has to be done about it. It is to be hoped that the present book will stimulate more people to take part in this thinking.

R. H. Thouless

Cambridge
12 December 1973.

[1] Dr Russell Targ, of the Stanford Research Institute, California.

Introduction

If there is one thing on which most serious workers in psychical research and the general public are in agreement it is on the very puzzling and paradoxical nature of precognition, which may be defined, in simple terms, as the extra-sensory perception of future events. Dr D. J. West, a former President of The Society for Psychical Research (the SPR), says in his book *Psychical Research Today* (Duckworth, 1954) that 'From a theoretical point of view the premonitory cases are the most extraordinary', and 'the stumbling block to all theories of ESP is precognition.' Professor H. H. Price, in his preface to Whately Carington's *Matter, Mind and Meaning* (Methuen, 1949) describes precognition as 'the most puzzling, perhaps, of all supernormal phenomena'. In an article in the *Hibbert Journal* in 1949 he said: 'Perhaps there is nothing in our whole experience queerer than precognition.' The late Professor C. D. Broad in the *Journal* of the SPR for December 1970 refers to ostensible precognition as 'much the most paradoxical of ostensibly paranormal phenomena.'

Indeed, precognition is so puzzling that most educated people, apart from those who have had personal experience of it, reject the phenomenon without giving it serious thought and all too often without studying the evidence for it. This book is an attempt to present the evidence for precognition in everyday life. I have not set out to prove that there is such a thing as precognition but simply to present some of the theories relating to it and to give a large number of cases, many of them sent to me by correspondents, so that readers can make up their own minds on the reality (or non-reality) of precognition. Almost all accounts are first hand, no account has been selected for publication without inquiries being made to clarify points that were not clear or to obtain more information and, whenever possible, corroborative evidence. Obviously, if I had not thought there was some element of ostensible precognition in a case I would not have published it. In certain cases, unless we assume collusion, lying, fraud or self-deception, the evidence for precognition seems to me to be strong. There are critics of psychical research who will grudgingly admit the value of evidence based on experimentation, although not without grumbles about the non-repeatability of experiments and dark hints of collusion between experimenter and subject, but will contemptuously dismiss the evidence of spontaneous cases on the grounds that it is merely 'anecdotal', with much emphasis being placed on the unreliability of human testimony, the frailty of memory, the tendency to embroider accounts and so on. So that the accounts in this book may be judged fairly I have given them as often as possible in the words of the people who have reported the cases, although some condensation has, of course, been necessary. This introduction is being written after the rest of the book has been completed, and the impression I have retained is that most of the accounts are written in simple, straightforward language without any attempt at embroidery. Because some cases are of a very personal nature I have provided pseudonyms at the request of the correspondent.

While I am on the subject of the alleged weakness of the 'anecdotal' evidence for precognition I should mention that many people believe that such evidence is confined to dreams and that as in any large city such as London, New York and Tokyo millions of people are dreaming every night some such dreams must come true. But is this the whole story? A precognitive experience can also take the form of a vision, an auditory or tactile hallucination, or a feeling of sadness or joy which can only be interpreted in the light of a later event and is not recognized at the time as being precognitive.

I am surprised that the strength of the evidence for precognition in its various forms in daily life is not generally realized, even by those, such as the late Mr W. H. Salter, for many years honorary secretary of the SPR, who have spent a lifetime in psychical research. In his book *Zoar* (Sidgwick and Jackson, 1961) Mr Salter said:

The evidence for precognition as a faculty of living minds is slight, if one leaves out of account the very curious phenomenon of forward displacement in card-guessing experiments, that is, the correct guessing not of the contemporary target, but of the next, or next but one, succeeding target. A considerable amount of evidence can now be quoted in support of this odd sort of occurrence but it has little apparent affinity with what we all mean by prediction. . . .

There are indeed a few interesting spontaneous cases of apparent foreknowledge – the pig, whom the bishop's wife dreamt she would find standing by the sideboard in the breakfast room, and there he was, has deservedly attained popular fame – but in general, the evidence for prediction, whether as a faculty of the living, or as purporting to originate with discarnate intelligences, is so slight that a discussion as to whether the second can be distinguished from the first is less profitable in the existing state of our knowledge, than a dispute would at present (October 1960) be as to whether Yetis are or are not members of the human species, since there are sufficient authentic human beings to serve as standards of comparison.

If such an experienced researcher as Mr Salter can take this view we should not be surprised if people of academic eminence in other fields ignore completely the possibility that precognition exists.

Dr John Beloff, Lecturer in Psychology at Edinburgh University and a member of the Council of the SPR, reviewing *The Nature of Mind* by A. J. P. Kenny, H. C. Longuet-Higgins, J. R. Lucas and C. H. Waddington (Edinburgh University Press, 1972) based on the first ten sessions of the Gifford Lectureships held in the academic year 1971–72, says in the *Journal* of the SPR for September 1973:

What . . . may perplex and dismay readers of this journal is why parapsychology is here so conspicuous by its absence. The one reference that I have been able to spot in the entire series comes in Longuet-Higgins's first address (p. 17) where, using the word clairvoyance in its vulgar sense to mean precognition, he points out that 'if anyone is genuinely clairvoyant (*sic.*) then modern physics is fundamentally in error. There are no two ways about it.' After that nothing. No one discussed whether precognition was a fact or not; the unspoken assumption on all sides was that the parapsychological evidence simply had not reached a stage yet where it need be taken seriously by educated men.

That four such outstanding intellectuals should in this day and age be able to discuss the nature of mind at such length without having to take account of the possibility of its possessing paranormal properties is a chastening reminder to us of how much work remains still to be done purely on the evidential level.

This book is my attempt to present some of the evidence found in spontaneous cases.

Now we turn to the evidence of the experimenter.

According to Dr Robert H. Thouless in his book *From Anecdote to Experiment in Psychical Research* (Routledge, 1972):

the experimental case for the reality of precognition has become much stronger in recent years, largely from experiments which had other objects than that of testing the reality of precognition. The precognitive design of experiment is a convenient one. For this reason, many of those engaged in *psi*-research (Schmeidler, Ryzl, Freeman and Nielsen among others) have elected to use the precognitive design of experiment and have found it no less fruitful than other methods of experimenting in ESP.[1]

It is worthwhile pointing out that in experiments to test the reality of precognition there is a very short interval, measured in seconds, between the guess and the result, which then has to be measured statistically – the experimenter does not rely on a single guess as the researcher into spontaneous cases does on a single case if the evidence is good enough. However, both methods of research complement each other and are equally necessary.

At this stage we should consider in more detail what is meant by precognition. I quote now from G. N. M. Tyrrell's book *Science and Psychical Phenomena* (Methuen, 1938). Tyrrell, who described precognition as 'the *direct* perception of events which have not yet taken place,' says:

We have first to note that cases may arise which look like precognition at first sight, but which may, in reality, have other explanations. If we take the activity of the subconscious mind into account, there are the following possibilities: (1) A person who makes a prediction may have subconsciously observed certain facts and drawn certain conclusions without being aware of it. All this may rise to consciousness in the form of a prediction and the prediction may be fulfilled because his subconscious inferences were sound. (2) A person may have formed a subconscious intention to do a certain thing and may have

[1] *psi* is the general term for extra-sensory perception and extra-sensorimotor activity.

subconsciously initiated a train of events likely to bring the thing about, and subconscious knowledge of this may rise to consciousness in the form of a prediction. (3) After a person has made a prediction from some cause or other, the fact of having made it may induce in him a subconscious desire to fulfil it, and he may unconsciously bring the fulfilment about. (4) Some human being unknown to the subject may have either drawn a correct inference about some future event, or may have formed an intention of bringing about some event, and this may be telepathically and subconsciously transferred to the subject, who may externalize it in the form of a prediction about the event. Some events, of course, are beyond the power of the subject to influence. In order to be genuine instances of foreknowledge, cases of precognition must be inexplicable under any of the above headings; and in considering the evidence, these possibilities should be borne in mind.

A distinction should be made between precognition as the foreseeing of an event which has not yet happened, such as the sinking of the *Titanic*, and the comparatively few cases where the object cognized already exists and it is only personal contact with it that lies in the future (examples are the Coptic rose and the unusual ceiling 'seen' by Mrs Hellström beforehand, described in chapter one, and the various cases of houses 'seen' in advance described in chapter eight). Possibly these two types of experience, both precognitive, should be described by different names, but I have found it difficult to think of suitable ones.

Under what circumstances does precognition occur?

Professor Ian Stevenson, of the University of Virginia, a writer of world reputation on parapsychology, says in a paper on precognition of disasters in the *Journal* of the American SPR published in April 1970 that 'the theme of precognitive experiences (as of most other spontaneous ESP experiences) are mostly serious and shocking events such as deaths and accidents. Comparatively few of these experiences have as their themes a trivial or pleasant event. Death is the commonest single event related to precognitive experiences.'

An opposing view is taken by Dr Louisa E. Rhine in *ESP in Life and Lab* (Collier-Macmillan):

One thread of similarity runs through all of the experiences that can more safely be taken to involve precognition: they are all *personalized* items. On this account the sweeping prognostications of great public events sometimes made seem not to fit the picture. In the first place they lack the 'intimate' quality of regular ESP topics, which is a first reason for doubt as to their ESP nature. But second and most important, they cannot be judged to be actually the product of precognitive ESP, even to the tentative degree which experiences involving small personal topics can. The factors for such judgement are lacking. Informed guessing and likely supposition cannot be ruled out, and vagueness of wording makes specific interpretation impossible.[2]

Something may be said for both viewpoints. There is strong evidence of precognition in experiences which preceded the sinking of the *Titanic*, to which I devote a chapter in this book, and the 1966 Aberfan disaster which I discussed in detail in *Frontiers of the Unknown* (Arthur Barker, London, 1968, and Popular Library, New York). On the other hand, there is a good deal of support in my present book for Dr Rhine's contention. I prefer to let readers draw their own conclusions, but some of the personalized items given by Mrs Eva Hellström in chapter one illustrate, I believe, what Dr Rhine had in mind in the passage I have just quoted.

I am encouraged in the view I have taken here by the experience of Mr J. B. Priestley who received over 1,000 letters – after that he stopped counting them – as the result of a BBC programme, *Monitor*, in which he appeared and at the end of which the interviewer, Huw Wheldon, appealed on his behalf to viewers to send him accounts of any experiences they had had that appeared to challenge the conventional and 'common sense' idea of time (I deal with this concept of 'common sense' in my final chapter).

Most of the letters were about dreams. Mr Priestley says in *Man and Time* (Doubleday, 1964) that 45 per cent of the precognitive dreams referred to deaths, terrible accidents and disasters of one sort and another and that another 45 per cent of them were concerned with trivialities, for which many of the writers apologized in advance.

'Clearly there is an enormous gap here,' says Mr Priestley. 'A whole range of living, between deathbeds and funerals at one end, holidays or shopping expeditions at the other, hardly makes an appearance in all these examples of precognition.' Women did

[2] Reprinted with permission of the Macmillan Publishing Co. Inc., New York. Copyright © Louisa E. Rhine, 1967.

not dream about their family life or happier sexual experiences and men, with a very few exceptions, described no precognitive dreams relating to their work.

The very things that interest most men – promotion or demotion, a new and difficult responsibility, trying another job, relations with head office or colleagues, all the battles, defeats or triumphs of a man's working life – are missing from their accounts of precognitive dreams. When we consider how much of a man's time is spent at work, how deeply he is concerned with it on any responsible level, how important its social and financial rewards may be to him, this absence of work dreams is astonishing.

From this Mr Priestley concludes that the precognitive dreaming of men and women does not offer us any reflection of people's main interests. 'It fails almostly completely,' he says, 'to represent this whole wide range of living. There is here in the middle some kind of barrier that is not there at the two extremes of the terrible and the trivial. Precognition exists – and of that I had no doubt long before these piles of letters were here – but only within these curious limitations.'

In my collection of cases I have found few precognitive experiences relating to happy events, either of men or women, and I cannot recollect a single one about a man's working life or office problems.

Now we turn to theories about precognition.

I was struck by a phrase in a review by Professor Bernard Williams of *Essays on J. L. Austin* (Oxford, 1973) in the *New Statesman* of 31 August 1973 (J. L. Austin, who died in 1960, was Professor of Moral Philosophy at Oxford). Mr Williams said: 'What he taught was a method, or set of methods, rather than a set of doctrines, and while he thought that there was a place for theories, if not in philosophy, at least as a result of it, he urged people to postpone theories until they had minutely examined large numbers of facts.'

I agree with this viewpoint completely. One of the strange things I have encountered in debates on radio or television is that people who have not made any study of psychical research express the strongest views on it. Ideally, I should postpone any discussion on theories of precognition until the final chapter, by which time the reader will have come to some conclusions of his own on a basis of a study of the evidence, but some outline is necessary at this stage.

In his admirable paper 'Supernormal Phenomena in Classical Antiquity' in the *Proceedings* of the SPR for March 1971, Professor E. R. Dodds says:

> Of all ostensibly supernormal phenomena precognition – defined by F. W. H. Myers as 'knowledge of impending events supernormally acquired' – has been in virtually all societies, from the most primitive to the most sophisticated, the most widely accepted in popular belief, and often also in the belief of educated men. Yet of all such phenomena it is probably the one of which it is hardest to give any rational account. The paradox of the situation was recognized in antiquity: Aristotle opens his discussion of the subject with the remark that it is difficult either to ignore the evidence or to believe it. Ostensible precognitions formed part of the accepted matter of history: the pages of nearly all ancient historians, from Herodotus to Ammianus Marcellinus, are full of omens, oracles, or precognitive dreams or visions. Yet how can an event in an as yet non-existent future causally determine an event in the present? This was already for Cicero, and even for his credulous brother Quintus, the *magna quaestio*, as it still is today.

Professor Dodds then goes on to say that modern theories of precognition fall into one or other of three broad categories. They attempt to evade or attenuate the paradox either (a) by juggling with the concept of time (Dunne, Saltmarsh, etc.); or (b) by trying where possible to re-interpret the phenomena in terms of unconscious inference from supernormally acquired knowledge of the present (Broad, Dobbs, Stevenson, etc.); or (c) by reversing the ostensible causal relationship and treating the precognitive experience as in some normal or supernormal ('psychokinetic') manner the cause of the subsequent event (Tanagras, Roll).

Let us consider the views of some of the authors in these three categories.

By far the best known is J. W. Dunne, author of *An Experiment with Time* (first published in 1927 and since then in paperback by Faber). Although Mr Dunne said that 'the general reader will find that the book demands from him no previous knowledge of science, mathematics, philosophy, or psychology [and] is considerably easier to understand than are, say, the rules of Contract Bridge', I have not found this to be so. The meaning of what Dunne is trying to say in *An Experiment with Time* and two of his other books, *The New Immortality* and *Nothing Dies* (both published by Faber), has always eluded me, so I will rely on a summary of his theory as given by H. F. Saltmarsh in a book I commend warmly, *Foreknowledge* (Bell, 1938).

Mr Saltmarsh says that Dunne, who was an aeronautical engineer, starts with the proposition that time has length. For example, it is four hours since I had breakfast, in another twelve hours it will be midnight, and so on. All these statements involve lengths of time.

On this view, the events of history are spaced out in a single dimension, along a line as it were.

But, he says, this is not all: time flows, we experience events in succession. It is as though the observer travels over the length of time and thus comes to one event after another.

Now, if time flows, it must flow at some particular rate: when we specify a rate of flow or other motion, we find that we require two factors, viz. length travelled over and time occupied in doing so. For example, my rate of walking is four miles an hour, or fifteen minutes per mile.

Thus if time flows over the 'length of time' there must be a second kind of time by which to rate the flow. This is what Mr Dunne calls Time 2. But we cannot stop here: Time 2 flows at a certain rate, which, of course, involves a Time 3, and so on to infinity.

Mr Dunne further argues that this infinite series of times would involve an infinite series of observers. He also draws many other conclusions and endeavours to show, with great ingenuity, and some plausibility, how this theory of serialism may be made to account for some odd and little understood phenomena; he even applies it to advanced physics and claims that it throws light in obscure places.

This ends Mr Saltmarsh's summary. He then adds that he does not accept Dunne's analysis of the nature of time and submits that his theory of serialism may be rejected on three general and easily understood grounds. Firstly, an infinite series of observers, even though those observers be only different levels of the consciousness of one person, and an infinite series of times, are unacceptable. Secondly, a time dimension cannot be changed into a space dimension, time and space being totally different in essential nature. Thirdly, the fundamental analysis is incorrect.

Time does not flow over a static history at a certain rate. History is that which is left behind by the onward surge of change. All rates or speeds are relativities, and time or change is the essential factor in them all.

Mr J. B. Priestley, while an admirer of Dunne for his insights on the time problem, questions some of his theories in *Man and Time*. He discussed these personally with Dunne a number of times, and says that at their last meeting he 'denounced his infinite regresses and begged him to abandon them. He did finally admit that the regresses would not do, and even suggested that they were a mere appearance, a kind of mirage on the unknown desert frontier, not to be crossed by the human intellect.' Still, Mr Priestley says that, until he looked through all the letters sent to him by way of the *Monitor* programme, he did not realize how many people had been reading Dunne. 'Without his examples, and his advice on the immediate recording of dreams, I suspect that at least a third of the best precognitive dreams I have been sent would never have come my way. Although it is not difficult to reject his general theory of serialism, he remains so far the most important figure in the campaign against the conventional idea of time.'

I also found that many of my correspondents had read Dunne's books on time.

We now turn to Mr Saltmarsh's theory of the greater specious present.

Mr Saltmarsh bases his theory on the conception, accepted in psychology, that the 'present moment' in which we perceive and act is not a mere point instant, but occupies a definite period of duration. Within the specious present there is no present, past or future, but there is a gradation with respect to clearness of apprehension of that which lies within its compass, maximum clearness corresponding with the centre of the specious present and a gradual reduction in clearness taking place towards its extremities.

Mr Saltmarsh likens the world to a bundle of approximately parallel wires seen through a slot, which moves in the direction of their length. All the wires are rigidly frozen in the past, the region over which the slot has passed, and some are frozen in the future, the region which the slot has not yet reached. Some, however, can be moved through the slot by the human percipient and actor, and the movement extends throughout the whole of their future length. Precognition is possible only with regard to future sections of the immovable wires. Free will acts alter the movable wires and thus, to some extent, the whole of the future.

'It is not easy to understand how, on this theory, any long-range prediction comes to be fulfilled in detail,' says Mr G. N. M. Tyrrell, who gives this summary of Saltmarsh's theory in *Science and Psychical Phenomena.*

I will leave category (b) alone for the present because I will shortly give in some detail Mr H. A. C. Dobbs's theory, and pass on to category (c) of Professor Dodds's classification as exemplified by the theories of Admiral Angelos Tanagras, Health Officer of the Greek Royal Navy and President of the Greek Society for Psychical Research, set out in *Psychophysical Elements in Parapsychological Traditions*, a parapsychological monograph published by the Parapsychology Foundation of New York in commemoration of the Admiral's ninetieth birthday on 20 May 1965. This monograph is a translation of Tanagras's book *Le Destin et la Chance: la Psychobolie humaine.*

The Admiral explains some hitherto inexplicable premonitions as the results of the workings of PK, or psychokinesis, which is the direct influence of mind on matter.

Let us imagine, for example, that as a result of natural anxiety in nervous people, one of such persons has a 'premonitory' dream of a car accident or a shipwreck just before starting on a journey. Let us also imagine that the person who had the dream (*or those people to whom it was told*) possesses telekinetic powers. As the impression of the dream is now in the subconscious, it tends to come true (Freud). And on the very spot indicated by the dream, at which, of course, the impression is most vivid, the telekinetic phenomenon is set in motion by the person concerned, *or by the others*, by means of a fault produced in the vehicle or an explosion on the boat. . . . In this way, the premonition is fulfilled. But it is not a case of premonition; it is simply a *telekinetic phenomenon.*

From this it seems that Admiral Tanagras considered that there is no true precognition. Indeed, he says in his first chapter:

Our object is to prove that there is no predetermination *in the details of life*, with which premonitions are most frequently concerned. In fact, although there is beginning and end, growth and decline, blossoming fructification and changes of season, these great laws are by no means revealed in a rigid and mathematically-strict fashion. On the contrary, they are dependent on a chain of other phenomena in nature which inevitably influence them. This is an essential point of our survey. Thus, evolution, alternating conditions, and the duration of each form of life depend in their details on thousands of other interdependent phenomena – on good or bad weather, on abundance or barrenness, and on all manner of accidents which may occur at any time.

If there is no such thing as predetermination in nature, what is the explanation of the numerous cases of premonition which have been fully verified? Admiral Tanagras asks at the opening of his second chapter.

A large number of premonitions could be explained, he says:
1 *By coincidence*, which can by no means be excluded.
2 *By telepathy*. Examples: thought transmission, in a dream, by malefactors preparing an evil deed which is carried out some days later; thought transmission by statesmen preparing for war, or by a professor whose thoughts, in preparing the questions for the following day, are transmitted to one of his students in sleep. It should be noted here that telepathic phenomena, in various forms, play an important part in premonitions.
3 *By clairvoyance*. Example: presentiment of some accident, for example, which must occur as the consequence of a cause already in existence; premonition of a disease which has not yet appeared but the germs of which already exist in the organism, etc.

Professor Stevenson, in his paper on precognition of disasters to which I have already referred, in reviewing the evidence for precognition in spontaneous cases with a foretelling of the future many years in advance and 'in certain experiments in which complicated methods far beyond ordinary knowledge or control are used to enter random tables for the selection of targets,' concludes from this that 'true precognition may occur *and may require some of the more recondite explanations that upset our habitual notions of causation and time*' (my italics).

We are now, I believe, coming closer to grips with the paradox and puzzle of precognition, and I turn to the theories of the late Mr H. A. C. Dobbs, as set out in his paper *Time and ESP* in the *Proceedings* of the SPR (vol. 54, pt 197, August 1965), to throw some light on the matter. Dobbs, a philosopher and mathematician, turned away from an academic career, for which he was admirably suited, to work in the Colonial Service and later in a 'hush hush' department of the Ministry of Defence. At Trinity

College, Cambridge, he was a favourite pupil of the late Professor C. D. Broad.

Dobbs postulated a two dimensional theory of time. It is almost impossible to summarize his paper, but I will attempt a brief outline to give some indication of his lines of thought.

In order to understand Dobbs's theory we need to know a certain amount about quantum mechanics which is the mechanics governing phenomena so small-scale that they cannot be described in classical terms.

Dobbs maintained that, in the ordinary one-dimensional theory of time, the only conceivable non-inferential form of precognition was the naïve one of direct acquaintance with a not yet existent future, 'which common sense and science rightly reject as logically and causally impossible.'

He believed there was a way of reconciling the kind of ostensibly precognitive results of the Soal-Shackleton experiments[3] with logic, common sense and science and it was by adopting a particular form of representative theory of ostensible precognition. This entailed the adoption of a theory of two-dimensional time (time as a complex variable) and of objective probability, in accordance with certain developments in modern theoretical physics. The developments he had in mind were associated with the Russian school of theoretical physics stemming from the work of V. A. Folk, N. S. Krylov and L. A. Khalfin, who investigated the time-energy uncertainty relationship of the Heisenberg Uncertainty Principle, by introducing a complex time conjugate to a complex energy (*Soviet Journal of Experimental and Theoretical Physics*, Vol. 17, 1947, p. 93). Dobbs says:

The essence of the theory I have been putting forward is that time is a complex variable, and not just a single real variable. According to the principles of quantum theory such an assumption implies that energy is also a complex variable, since time and energy are complementary quantities in the sense of Heisenberg's Uncertainty Principle. This is exactly the position taken up by the School of Russian physicists to whom I have referred. Again following the Russian School I conceive of virtual interactions which have physical effects between particles of real rest mass (such as protons, electrons and molecules of ordinary matter) and particles of imaginary mass. Such interactions

[3] *Proc.* SPR xlvii, 1943, pp. 21-150.

will be perfectly frictionless and reversible, and it will therefore be possible for two human brains to exchange particles of imaginary mass without the magnitudes of such interactions being in any way attenuated by spatial separation or distance. In these interactions between brains and the particles of imaginary rest mass, which I will call psitrons, travelling without any form of attenuation through friction or resistance in the intervening space, you have the physical mechanism required for ostensible precognition. These will be available to give a 'causal' explanation of the direct acquaintance with the objective probabilities of event outcomes still in the future.

It will be noticed that Mr Dobbs refers to 'objective probabilities'. I have dealt with his theory at some length because it meets the objections of those readers who might entertain the notion of precognition, if they give it any thought at all, but for their built-in objection to any conception of a future which, they believed, contained events fixed in advance. 'You can't do anything about it; it's fixed in advance', or 'It's Fate', sums up the resigned attitude of many people to events in the future, and it is this attitude which invites rebellion.

But modern physics speaks of probabilities, not certainties, and Dobbs, in support of his theory, points out that on a classical-physical deterministic world-view a strict application of the laws to *exact* initial conditions yields *certainties* not probabilities. 'Thus no ostensible precognition reached in this way could ever be falsified which is contrary to fact: as shown for example by cases where the precognizing percipient deliberately intervenes to falsify the ostensible precognition,' he states.

Dobbs quotes 'the famous case of Lady Z and her toppling coachman' as one of a number of well-attested instances which show that no theory of ostensible precognition which yields certainties derived by inference is tenable.

This case concerns a Lady Z who dreamed of driving in a street near Piccadilly and of her coachman falling off the box on to his head in the road, crushing in his hat. Next day, wishing to go to Woolwich, she gave orders to her coachman to start at ten o'clock, though, on account of her dream, she half hoped for an excuse to go by train. He demurred at starting at the time proposed but said that by eleven o'clock he and the horses would be fit for the journey. Lady Z was driven to Woolwich without incident; on the return journey, when reaching Piccadilly, she noticed that the drivers of other vehicles were looking at her coachman. She then saw that he was leaning back on the box as though the horses were pulling violently. The carriage turned up Down Street and Lady Z suddenly remembered her dream. She called to the coachman to stop, jumped out and caught hold of her child, who was with her. She then called to a policeman to catch the coachman, who was swaying in his seat. Just as she did so, the coachman fell off the box. Had Lady Z been less prompt in calling assistance, he would probably have fallen exactly as she had seen in her dream.

H. F. Saltmarsh discusses this case and others in which warnings were conveyed in dreams in his book *Foreknowledge* and comments:

> the interesting point about all these cases is that, while the course of future events appears to have been foreseen, those events are not inexorably fixed but are capable of being modified by deliberate action beforehand. It might be put this way: the future foreseen is what might, and most probably would happen if things were left to run their course, but in actual fact does not happen because of the intervention of someone who steps in and performs some action which averts the complete fulfilment of the precognition.

But sometimes intervention cannot be made. A lady who is a member of the SPR and who has had a number of interesting precognitive experiences, had a vivid short dream in 1966 concerning herself. Written on a banner held up to her in rust-red letters in a very angular hand were these words: 'Your death will be at the age of –' (the year was to be 1969). This dream was repeated several times later although in a different way. She became 'very alarmed and distressed', and put her affairs in order as far as possible. 'I was haunted by it,' she wrote to me (I later interviewed her).

In 1967 she had the feeling, while driving in a car, that she would be reprieved. However, in 1969 she had a very bad fall in the hall of her flat, breaking her right hip. She had to have an operation. 'I have been very ill since and twice near death in the last two years,' she said. 'The dream was a warning, but only partly right. However, it was very nearly right. And I still live under its shadow.'

Now the stage is set for consideration of the cases. The best cases, from an evidential viewpoint, are those in which the experience is recorded in diary form and dated and witnessed, as in Mrs Hellström's experiences in chapter one, or sent to an experienced investigator in advance as was done by Dame Edith Lyttelton, whose experiences are given in chapter two. Next best are cases in which some reliable person was told about the experience *before* the ostensible fulfilment of it; there are many such cases in my book. In many other cases no evidence in confirmation is possible because the person who had the experience was alone at the time or because some person who could have confirmed it is dead or could not be traced or was in a distant land. In such cases I have had to use my judgement on the genuineness of the account before deciding to publish it. The person who stands up to repeated questioning about an experience obviously believes in the truth of it. Modern cases are to be preferred to old ones because there is less chance here of faults of memory affecting the narrative.

One last word is necessary. Throughout the book there are references to hallucinations of various kinds and they should not be interpreted as false perceptions in the sense that so many psychiatrists use the term (I am stating this on the advice of a well-known consultant psychiatrist). An illusion, of course, is a false perception, and is different again from a delusion, which is a false opinion about a matter of fact which need not necessarily involve, though it often does involve, false perception of sensible things.

That great American psychologist, Professor William James, said that hallucinations are often talked of as mental images projected outwards by mistake. 'But when an hallucination is complete it is much more than a mental image,' says James in his *Principles of Psychology* (Macmillan, 1890). 'An hallucination is a strictly sensational form of consciousness, as good and true a sensation as if there were a real object there. The object happens not to be there, that is all.'

James also mentions that the hallucination sometimes carries a change of the general consciousness with it, so as to appear more like a general lapse into a dream. I do not like the use of the word 'hallucination' but one must use it for want of a better one. I would like to add just one word to Professor James's last sentence in the paragraph above, so that it reads: 'The object happens not to be there *physically*, that is all.' But it is there in a real sense to the percipient who, for purposes of this definition should be understood to be someone in good mental and physical health who has not taken alcohol or drugs before the experience occurred.[4]

[4] In this introduction I have quoted Dr Thouless's views on the experimental case for the reality of precognition. Since the book went to the printer *The Encyclopedia of the Unexplained* (Routledge, 1974), has been published and in it Dr J. B. Rhine classes the evidence for precognition as conclusive. Dr Rhine is, of course, best known for his experimental work.

1 The case of the Coptic rose

In 1947 Mrs Eva Hellström, one of the founders of the Swedish Society for Psychical Research, was on the point of going to sleep in her home in Stockholm, when suddenly she 'saw' at the end of her bed what seemed to be a type of church garment so extraordinary that she could not imagine there could be a counterpart to it in reality. It looked like a long simple white shirt of cotton material with a beautiful richly embroidered round yoke in many colours but mostly red and gold. On the front there were two small lions embroidered in gold, one on each side of the opening.

The following morning Mrs Hellström made a sketch of the visionary garment, but she was unable to draw the lions. As she had a strong conviction that this hallucination had a special meaning she told her husband, Dr Bo Hellström, a consultant hydro-electric engineer who had been travelling all over the world since 1925 in the course of his work, and two friends what she had seen, and made a note of it in a small diary which she always kept in her handbag.

The fulfilment of Mrs Hellström's precognitive experience came on 8 February 1951 when she visited the Coptic Museum in Cairo and was taken by the Director, Professor Labibe, to the second floor where there was a room for textiles and old clerical garments and bishops' requisites. They were all like the garment she had sketched: white wide shirts, some with embroideries on the upper part, with a lot of red; some with loose red sleeves in silk with gold and silver embroidery. Professor Labibe also showed her a large collar of gold thread, or something similar, embroidered with many semi-precious stones in different colours.

When Mrs Hellström visited the museum a few days later she was told by Professor Labibe that the collar was that of a Coptic bishop from Ethiopia. There were no lions on the collar in the museum, but lions were the symbol for Ethiopia and the Emperor of Ethiopia was called the Lion of Judah and had a lion in his coat of arms.

Dr Hellström signed a statement that he was again shown the drawing of the Coptic collar and garment when at the Taj Mahal, India, on 14 January 1951, three weeks before the visit to the museum in Cairo.

Mrs Hellström's case book contains a letter from a friend stating that she had been shown a sketch of something which she (Mrs Hellström) had thought was a church garment during the autumn of 1947 and had been told that she had seen this garment in a vision. The sketch was in the centre of the paper which Professor Hellström had certified on 14 January 1951.

It was at this museum that Dr Hellström had earlier had the first evidence which he accepted of his wife's paranormal powers. This concerned the case of the Coptic rose which I will give later in this chapter. Mrs Hellström says in her two case books deposited in the library of the SPR in London: 'When I first had my ESP experiences my husband thought them to be pure imaginations but since the finding of the Coptic rose in Cairo (in 1949) he has been convinced about the phenomena and has taken an interest in them, though he has never had the time to study the subject. After all, he is a Doctor of Technology, not of Psychology! I am quite sure that my strongest motivation has been to convince my husband – perhaps make an impression on him.' Dr Hellström died in 1967.

Mrs Hellström, who was born in September 1898, married when she was nineteen and had four children, was for a time interested in Spiritualism, but, as she points out in the introduction to her first case book, 'I soon found that the Spiritualistic movement was not for me. I didn't like the way they made it a religious sect. I understood that many of the phenomena could be explained in other ways. Being the daughter, sister, wife and mother of scientists, it did not satisfy me to believe only – I wanted to study and investigate. In my country most Spiritualists are all against people who want to investigate under scientific conditions and to take precautions in the séance room.'

However, Mrs Hellström was still interested in Spiritualism when she went to London in the spring of 1947 and there had her first visions or hallucinations. She was then forty-eight. Very often when she experienced these visions she had a dizzying feeling in the pit of her stomach which made her feel that she had become lighter in weight. Also, she used to wake up with a jerk as if she was falling. Quite frequently these visions came during an attack of migraine for which she took tablets containing caffeine and rested.

One night when she was lying in bed in a relaxed state, although wide awake, Mrs Hellström suddenly 'saw' a small miniature in beautiful colours about three yards in front of her. It was a portrait of a man in a fifteenth-century costume with puffed sleeves and a big white pleated collar. Then the vision changed and she 'saw' what appeared to be a fragment of an old sculptured ceiling in beautiful old oak. The next evening she 'saw' again a vision in delightful pastel shades, pearl-grey and rose. The scene was outside a convent where nuns in long veils bent down to help sick people to get up from the ground. At the same time she had the intuition that this meant 'Bear ye one another's burdens.' Of the seventeen hallucinations which she had that year (1947) all were miniatures except the one of the garment containing the collar of the Ethiopian bishop, which was in natural size.

In the autumn of 1947 Mrs Hellström became a member of the SPR in London, bought all the Society's proceedings and journals, and that year took the initiative in forming a Society for Psychical Research in Stockholm. For more than twenty years she was the honorary secretary of this society.

Now for the case of the Coptic rose.

In 1949 Dr Hellström was called to Egypt on an important mission. He had been there before but his wife had not and they decided that she should go with him. There was so much to arrange in a hurry for the family and for the journey that Mrs Hellström had no time to read anything about Egypt, its history or the customs of the country before they set out. Her youngest son was to accompany her to Florence and stay with relatives there while she went to Rome to meet her husband.

Mrs Hellström and her son started on their journey on 13 December from Copenhagen in a comfortable tourist bus. On the third day of their journey they travelled from Wildungen to Basle by way of Heidelberg, where they had lunch at an old students' inn. Mrs Hellström's father, who died in 1932, had at one time studied in Heidelberg, so naturally he was in her thoughts while she was there. At that time she had been having visions of her father.

When they left Heidelberg it was quite dark and Mrs Hellström dozed off for a while in the bus. When she began to wake up she 'saw' a coloured picture of her father. In her account of it, she says:

A little sceptically I thought to myself: 'Well, here I am in the neighbourhood of Heidelberg, and so my subconscious makes up a picture of my father; that is quite natural'. But then I suddenly had an hallucination of an entirely unexpected picture. It was like some kind of painting with a beautiful pattern. In a strange way it was clearly illuminated, and I realized that this was something that I had never experienced before. For the first time in my life I felt the conviction that this was a precognition and that I would find the original of the picture on my journey.

I got the impression that the picture was some twenty-five by thirty centimetres and it was in colours. What impressed me most was the dark rich pink background and the centre figure, which looked like four hearts meeting in the middle. There were also some black ornaments which I did not have time to register properly, but they appeared to be a kind of spiral located at the four corners. They ran between the hearts into the centre. Because I felt the strong conviction that this was a precognition and that I was going to find the original of the picture on my journey, I immediately took out a little notepad which I always carry in my handbag and made a sketch from memory. This was far from easy in the swaying bus, and it was almost dark. I did this for my own sake as an aid to memory – everybody knows how quickly dreams are dissolved. On the sketch I also wrote in Swedish that the picture had a rose background and that the ornaments were black. I drew the four hearts and indicated the two spirals at each corner. I wondered very much, however, if I was to find this picture in Egypt, since it rather resembled old Swedish peasant art and had nothing Egyptian about it: for instance, dancers or lotus flowers as one might have expected.

We stayed for the night in Basle, and I showed the sketch to my son and to the young bus hostess, with whom we were on very friendly terms. They were the first persons to see my sketch. Later I received a letter from this Fräulein B. in which she testifies to having seen the sketch in Basle and says that she remembers it very well.

I left my son in Florence, met my husband in Rome and went on with him to Cairo. . . . After a few days in Cairo I met two Swedish ladies, Dr T. and Professor B. I soon found out that they were both interested in parapsychology. I told them about my vision, showed them my sketch and asked them if they, who had lived in Cairo for more than twenty years, could tell me where to look for my picture. But they had no idea where it might be or what it represented. I have testimonials from them both that I showed them my sketch on 27 December, two days before we actually found the original.

On the last day but one in Cairo Dr T. suggested that we should visit the Coptic Museum on the following day as she held it to be one of the most beautiful sights of the town. . . . On 29 December we were picked up by Mr and Mrs A. who took us to the museum in their car (I must admit that neither my husband nor myself had the faintest idea that such a museum existed and personally I did not know that the Copts were the Christians in Egypt). When we all met outside the museum – we were six in the party – Dr T. whispered to me that in the night she had had the feeling that I was to find my picture in the Coptic Museum. The Coptic Museum has a collection of wonderful ancient relics and fragments from the first Christian Churches and monasteries in Egypt. The Christian community was founded by the apostle Marcus who came to Alexandria in the year AD 65. The museum is full of wooden figures, ikons, sculptures and ornaments, most of them carved out of sandstone or chalk.

When we entered the second room Dr T. grabbed my arm and exclaimed 'Eva, there is your picture'. It was a stone slab. I was dumbfounded. I took out my little pad and held up the sketch beside the stone slab. There was no doubt about it; all the other five persons immediately realized that this was the original picture which my sketch showed. My husband took a snapshot of it. In the middle there was a four-leaved clover in the shape of a cross. I was told that it probably represented what is locally known as the 'Coptic rose', a simple rose which in the old days was cultivated in the Coptic monasteries, and the picture contains many Christian symbols.

Mrs Hellström said that the size of the slab which she had estimated at twenty-five by thirty centimetres turned out to be forty-three by forty-eight centimetres. She had thus estimated the proportions correctly but to a smaller scale.

What she had not noticed was the existence of a small circle in the centre and four long slender sepals, but, she remarked, 'who can remember all the details of a pattern which one sees for only a few seconds?'

Her account continues:

The strangest thing about this hallucination is, however, the colour. I had seen the picture in my vision as having a background of rich pink and with black ornaments. When we found the original there was hardly any colour left: it had been worn off by time. There were some remnants of black on the frame and on one of the petals. We were not sure about the pink colouring. We thought we found some very faint traces, but as the stone was in itself a faint yellow-pinkish shade it was difficult to say. I go so far as to say that I should never have recognized the stone slab myself because to me the colours were the most outstanding elements and I was looking specially for them but they did not exist any more. Dr T. who had only seen my sketch in black and white recognized the pattern on the slab because she did not miss the colours. She and Professor B. wrote their names across the sketch to verify that I had shown them the sketch two days earlier.

Mrs Hellström later met the director of the museum, Mr Osman R. Rostem (this was before the appointment of Professor Labibe) and she also corresponded with him. He told her that the slab appeared to have been pink and black when it was new, perhaps a thousand years ago. He sent her a diagram of the remnants of colour which can still be seen.

Mr Rostem also said that the stone slab had never been reproduced, so she could not have seen it beforehand.

Mrs Hellström's conclusion follows:

What I said at the beginning of this narrative, viz. that time and space seem to lose all reality during experiences of this kind, applies very much to this case. I saw the hallucination of the stone slab sixteen days before I actually found the original in Cairo. When I found it I saw the slab as it looked in 1949, without colours. But in my vision I had seen it as it must have been a thousand years earlier.

I would like to finish by pointing out another peculiar causal connection in this case which has repeated itself in a few more of my cases. I found the original only because I had made my little sketch of the hallucination and had shown it to several people beforehand. One of these persons took me to a museum which I had not even known existed. Then she pointed out the original to me which I would never have found without her. I was like a chess piece being moved around in a game of chess.

The 'Dr T.' of this narrative was Dr Vivi Täckholm, Professor of Botany at the Fouad I University, Cairo. She said in a statement that she was shown Mrs Hellström's drawing in her notebook on 27 December and at that moment she could not imagine what it was. On the following day she told Dr and Mrs Hellström about the Coptic Museum and said that they should not leave Cairo without visiting it. They had not heard about the museum before this.

During the night that followed Dr Täckholm dreamt that the original of Mrs Hellström's drawing was in the Coptic Museum and she told her so in the morning before entering the museum.

The director certified that the museum did not contain any other example showing the same pattern or design as the slab.

Mrs Hellström said that a psychical researcher in London who had investigated this case some years ago asked her if she thought that the resemblance between her sketch and the stone slab was so striking that she could rule out chance coincidence. After all, there were slight differences. For instance, in her sketch the circle in the centre was missing.

She replied that when she visited Cairo some years after this experience she went to the Coptic Museum and met the new director, Professor Labibe, showing him her sketch without telling him anything about it. 'Oh yes, that is the slab from room number nine,' he said.

'I think that this is the best answer I can give to the question about chance coincidence,' Mrs Hellström commented.

This is a very well documented case. The only question we are called on to decide is whether the design 'seen' by Mrs Hellström in her vision in the bus was the same as that of the Coptic rose in the museum in Cairo. There is certainly a very strong resemblance between the two, as can be seen by comparing Mrs Hellström's sketch with her husband's photograph of the slab in the case book. When we remember that the slab had never been photographed before this, that the museum did not contain any other object showing the same pattern or design, and that the original colours of the slab were those 'seen' by Mrs Hellström, I believe we can accept that the resemblance has been established.

An unusual feature of this case is Dr Täckholm's dream that the original of Mrs Hellström's drawing would be found in the Coptic Museum. We must bear in mind that Dr Täckholm had previously visited the museum – as Mrs Hellström had not – and may have noticed the slab without remembering that she had done so. If so, this information could have emerged in her dream, but this does not, of course, invalidate Mrs Hellström's precognitive experience. As she had 'seen' the Coptic rose in its original colours in her vision retrocognition was also involved in this experience.

An unusual feature about the next case I will give from Mrs Hellström's collection is that details of the ostensible precognition of a collision between a tram and a train in Sweden were sent to Dr J. B. Rhine and a few other scientists long before the accident happened.

In her diary of 26 March 1954, Mrs Hellström made the following entry:

I dreamt this morning of a tram accident. The dream had the character of precognition and was in colours. But I can't understand how it can come true because it was a smash between a tram and a green underground carriage or several.

I had the feeling that Bo (my husband) and I were flying over Stockholm. I looked down, thought that we were somewhere in the neighbourhood of Kungsträdgården. While I was looking down an accident happened there. In the dream I said to myself: 'The green one ran into No. 4 from the back. There was a motor car and it was his fault.' I saw an ordinary blue tram of the type that No. 4 has, and a green train, looking something like the underground trains, run into the tram from the back. Possibly there were several green carriages. When they had smashed, the green carriages were driven to one side by the speed, and placed themselves at right angles to the tram No. 4. A clumsy driver of a motor car was the cause of the accident.

Then in the dream I went to a policeman and told him that if he wanted a witness I was willing to give evidence that the motor (car) driver caused the accident. I thought the policeman was standing in Kungsträdgården. Kungsträdgården might have been symbolic for Stockholm. Perhaps I also saw the Royal Palace and other buildings but do not remember this.

Mrs Hellström made a sketch of the accident 'seen' in her dream. This was verified by her husband.

At the time there were no green trains in Stockholm except on the underground and tram No. 4 was the only new type tram. During the following month Mrs Hellström was invited to visit a friend in Djursholm, a suburb of Stockholm, and was surprised to notice that the train included one green carriage. She was told by the conductor that the railway company had ordered five or six such green cars and that this one was the first. Before this the carriages had always been painted in different shades of brown.

On 4 March 1956, after the Djursholm Railway Company had introduced new green carriages, a collision occurred at Valhallavägen between a train of this company and a tram No. 4. The tram driver blamed the failure of his brakes for the accident in which his tram hit the middle of the train. The tram left the rails, as did the middle carriage of the train. There were no casualties.

The positions of the railway carriage and the tram after the accident were similar to those sketched by Mrs Hellström after her dream two years earlier.

Mrs Hellström obtained a statement from an official of the railway company that although the Djursholm trains had several times run into cars, there had not been a collision between a train and a tram since he had started working for the company in 1923.

But what about the driver of the car who, in Mrs Hellström's dream, caused the accident?

He was, in fact, an intruder from an earlier accident, one she had witnessed in London in 1930-32 when, after going to a theatre, she drove for a long while after a drunken driver who 'hogged' the road and eventually overturned his car. Mrs Hellström went to a policeman and told him that if he wanted a witness she was willing to give evidence against the man.

Mrs Hellström said in her case book: 'When I had the dream about the tram-train accident it struck me as strange that the dream resembled the accident in England, but since I experienced the first part of my dream in exactly the same way as the second part, e.g. I "saw" everything in colours as I always do in these dreams, I never suspected that one part could be a precognition and the other part a retrocognition.'

It will be remembered that retrocognition was also involved in Mrs Hellström's vision which preceded the finding of the Coptic rose.

She remarked in her notes on this case that in her precognitive dreams the colour always has a significant meaning.

She also remarked: 'Another observation I have made is that when I get a precognitive dream the details at the beginning of the dream very often are right when the happening occurs. At the end of the dream, however, when the conscious mind gradually returns, the details sometimes become vague and indistinct and will very likely turn out to be wrong. Probably pictures from memory and imagination rise when one is gradually awaking.'

There is confirmation for Mrs Hellström's viewpoint in an observation made by Professor C. D. Broad in his chapter on precognition in *Science and ESP* (Routledge, 1967). He says that when there is a preperception of a certain event or state of affairs, which is afterwards realized, it will seldom correspond accurately in all its details. 'It will generally be supplemented, and often distorted, by features due to the experient's past experiences and acquired associations, his present situation and interests, and so on.'

Mrs Hellström later discovered from a friend that on 24 March 1954, two days before she had her dream, the newspaper *Dagens Nyheter* had carried a photograph and news item about the new green railway carriage.

'I am positive that I had not seen it, but perhaps my subconscious had', she said in her account of this case.

However, she also states that she did not have this newspaper in her home, so I think it is very unlikely that she had seen this particular picture.

Mrs Hellström also points out that no accident between the Djursholm train and the number 4 tram could ever happen again as the train now stopped at a station before the point of collision. 'Accordingly this accident was the only collision which had in those days occurred between the train and the tram and the only collision that can ever occur. From a statistical point of view this is important.'

I feel that we can agree with this observation.

Another precognitive experience concerning a train accident is noted in Mrs Hellström's diary under the date of 28 March 1953:

> Last night I had a dream which I think may be a precognition. I was on board a train in a tunnel. There was probably a poisonous gas or smoke, the train was standing still and when I was descending from the train there were lots of people lying on the ground along the train in the tunnel, probably dead, at least unconscious. All were lying higgeldy-piggeldy, but nobody was injured. I can't imagine what had happened.

Five days later, on 2 April, an accident occurred in Stockholm's new underground, the very first accident there, Mrs Hellström observes. No one was injured, but when the train ran through a wall of mortar, and the brakes were applied, a number of people fell to the floor of the carriage. The tunnel was filled with smoke and a great deal of dust.

Mrs Hellström remarked in her case book that the only item in her dream which did not coincide with what happened in the accident five days later was that she saw people lying in the tunnel whereas they were lying on the floor of the carriages after the accident. A daughter of her best friend since childhood was travelling in the train involved in the accident. Of the six precognitions about accidents which she had had up to that date, this was the only one in which she knew one of the persons involved in the accident.

In her precognitive experiences about accidents, Mrs Hellström noted, she seems to have arrived on the scene just after the accident had occurred.

Another of Mrs Hellström's dreams or visions about accidents that were yet to happen concerned a man who was killed in a fall from a roof.

On 5 August 1952, when she was at Skodsborg, Denmark, Mrs Hellström wrote in her diary: 'I dreamt that I was walking on something that looked like a flat roof. Perhaps with a low barrier or something of the sort. Saw a person (man) fall down from the roof. Saw him floating in the air. Died. It was high, made of stone. Wasn't quite sure but I imagined that there was also somebody else round about who perhaps may have pushed him down? I am not sure, rather unclear.'

A man named Rune Nilsson fell to his death from the roof of the gasworks at Värtan on 8 December 1952. Mrs Hellström visited the works and spoke to an engineer about the case. She established from the police report that Nilsson, who had been painting at the time of the accident, had fallen from the roof of the coke conveyor tunnel, which was flat.

Scaffolding or bracing was visible in a picture of the site of the accident in a newspaper and this could have appeared to her like a low barrier.

Nilsson fell from a height of eighteen metres and died twelve hours later. The building from which he fell was made of bricks.

It will be noticed that there are strong points of resemblance between what Mrs Hellström experienced in her dream and what occurred when Rune Nilsson fell to his death four months later.

Mrs Hellström wrote in her case book:

In the police report it is clear that other workmen were in the neighbourhood, even if not on the roof of the coke conveyor. I didn't see anybody there either, only had an impression that there were people nearby. It is said in the report that Nilsson seems to have hit his head on a roof truss and at the same time as he fell down a board fell down and placed itself right over Nilsson's body. These facts were vaguely noticed by me but were interpreted incorrectly. I went to the police station to arrive at an understanding of the unpleasant, vague feeling that Nilsson had been pushed down. I got a satisfying explanation.

Mrs Hellström's comment on her incorrect interpretation of what she saw in her dream is worth noting. Another sensitive once told me that she has noticed the errors that can come into an account of an experience when the conscious mind takes over and starts interpreting material that has emerged from the subconscious.

On 24 January 1953, Mrs Hellström was sitting at her sewing machine doing some mending when, according to her diary: 'Suddenly, like a flash of lightning, I saw a vision of myself walking in a street in Cairo. I am convinced that Bo and I will be going there soon. Bo says point blank "No." He will begin lecturing on 9 February and the lectures go on for six weeks. Then, he says, it will be too hot for Cairo. He doesn't want to go.'

Mrs Hellström noted that this experience was of quite a new type, as sudden and unexpected as the visions, but what she saw was like a film in grey and white within her and not like the 'ordinary' external visions.

Later in the day Mrs Hellström woke up after a nap and saw in colours 'a kind of beetle or scarab'. She sketched it in her diary and wrote: 'Wonder what it symbolizes?'

Dr and Mrs Hellström were unexpectedly invited to Ethiopia on 3 February 1954. On their return journey they arrived in Cairo on 26 February and stayed there a few days.

It will be noted that Mrs Hellström was convinced that she would be going 'soon' to Cairo with her husband, but the journey took place thirteen months later. This suggests that in some experiences it is difficult to estimate the time element involved.

The scarab, I feel, could be taken as a symbol for Egypt. Symbolism was involved in some of Mrs Hellström's other experiences. For instance, she noted in her diary on 4 February 1954 that while resting in the afternoon she 'saw' a beautiful sunlit winter landscape with a skier and a church. At seven o'clock that evening her sister Astrid telephoned to say that her husband, General Ivar Holmquist, was going to have another operation in a few days. She wrote in her diary: 'I believe now that Ivar was the skier who went skiing to the church.'

General Holmquist, who was Army Chief during the war, was known as Sweden's skiing general. He had been operated on for cancer in the rectum in 1950 and had been quite well since then. With his wife he had been skiing in the mountains for almost a month but on his return had developed bladder trouble for which he consulted a doctor at hospital. On the day when Mrs Hellström had her vision the general was told that the cancer probably had spread and he would have to have another operation.

Four days later she commented in her diary: 'I think it was an extremely beautiful vision telling that his (General Holmquist's) time was out now when I saw him skiing to church in the sunlit ski track, especially as he was a deeply religious person'.

General Holmquist died on 24 September 1954.

Some of Mrs Hellström's precognitive experiences concerned more pleasant topics than accidents or death.

For instance, in her diary for 22 November 1952, she wrote: 'Yesterday, when I was resting, I saw a vision or had a dream or both combined. The first part of it I forgot at once – I think it had to do with a lot of white horses in a cluster doing something. I was there with them. Then all of a sudden – I remember this part very clearly – a big white horse ran along the road at full gallop or runaway with flying mane. . . . It ran away from me.'

Mrs Hellström accompanied the entry with a sketch showing her position as observer and that of the horse.

On the evening of 23 November – forty-eight hours after the dream or visionary experience – Mrs Hellström went with her daughter Margareta Armfelt-Hansell to see the film *Viva Zapata*. The cinema had a few pictures from the film outside, including some of men on horses, but none of a horse without a rider and none of the runaway horse galloping along a road.

During the film Mrs Hellström noticed that there were white horses in it. She said to her daughter, 'I saw a vision yesterday with a white horse. If that scene comes in this film, I will give you a push. Then you must help me remember what happens in the film.' When the scene came with the runaway horse Mrs Hellström gave her daughter a push and cried out, 'There is my horse.'

On their return to the house Mrs Hellström showed her daughter, and also her husband, the entry in the diary and the sketch of the runaway horse.

Both certified the correctness of this report.

A somewhat similar experience concerning the theatre occurred during the afternoon of 10 November 1961. Mrs Hellström had been sleeping but woke to see a vision in colour of a big ballroom where a crowd of teenagers were dancing. The girls wore brightly coloured dresses including some in turquoise-blue and cerise. She also seemed to see something coloured above their heads, 'either some kind of paper hat or head dress or balloons or maybe coloured lanterns'.

Mrs Hellström had planned a trip with her husband to London and told him about her experience before they started (he verified this).

Four days later Dr and Mrs Hellström and a friend, Mr Victor Jansa, saw the musical play, *Bye Bye Birdie*, at Her Majesty's Theatre, London. Half way through the first act Mrs Hellström pushed her husband's arm and whispered, 'Look, here is the ballroom scene with the youngsters.'

Some of the girls wore cerise-coloured dresses and others were in turquoise-blue. There was something above their heads but Mrs Hellström could not see what it was. Dr Hellström left the theatre because he was not feeling well. In the interval Mrs Hellström told Mr Jansa about her vision.

'When we came back to the hotel I made him come with me into our bedroom, where my husband was in bed. I unlocked my suitcase, took out my diary and read the account to them both. They agreed that the scene had been quite in accordance with my account.'

Dr Hellström and Mr Jansa added their signatures certifying that this entry in Mrs Hellström's diary was correct in every detail.

The following day Mrs Hellström went to a matinée at the theatre. She noticed then that two of the girls in the cast wore caps with big cerise-coloured woollen tufts at the top which showed above the heads of the crowd. Two other girls waved above their heads wands with long paper streamers in red and white at the top.

Mrs Hellström's two case books contain details of 239 cases which she experienced between 1947 and 1964 (there is a single case relating to 1938). I have read all of them carefully and assess those with some degree of precognition involved as amounting to slightly more than sixty. It is significant that in two-thirds of the cases (42) the information came in the form of visions in colour, almost always after a period of rest. In thirteen instances the precognitive experience occurred in the course of a dream and a few experiences were described by Mrs Hellström as a dream and vision combined. There were several auditory experiences involving ostensible precognition. In an account of one of her cases Mrs Hellström said: 'When I have heard a voice speak sometimes, it has almost every time been about precognitions. Then it has always been an impersonal voice unknown to me.'

This impersonal element was also a factor in Mrs Hellström's precognitive dreams. In her introduction to the cases she said:

> When I have these precognitive dreams there is a very definite difference from my ordinary dreams: that is why I know. In my ordinary dreams I play the leading part, I am the centre of the proceedings. I take an active part in the drama. I am in love, I suffer, I am jealous, I run away from something, I am afraid, I wake up in tears. I had these dreams many times when I was younger, also many years after I was married. As far as I have been able to remember these dreams are not in colours. My precognitive dreams are always in colours. The colour is often of great importance for the case [Mrs Hellström gives as an instance of this the collision between a green train and a tram]. Very often in my visions as well [an example here is the case of the Coptic rose]. I am only an observer in the precognitive dreams. I walk about watching what is happening to other people, but I am not a bit emotionally engaged.

Mrs Hellström said she had also had a few precognitions in which she seemed to have identified herself with somebody else who was involved in an accident.

The time element in Mrs Hellström's cases varied greatly.

Very occasionally the precognitive experience was fulfilled the same day, more often there was an interval of days, but quite frequently weeks or months divided the experience from the fulfilment of it, and in some cases the interval was one of several years. For instance, the case with which I opened this chapter, that of the collar of the Coptic bishop, involved a time interval of four years. Another case with a long time gap between the experience and the fulfilment of the precognitive element in it concerned a ceiling 'seen' by Mrs Hellström in a train in which she was travelling with her husband in India in January 1951. She sketched the design, made a note of the colours and the fact that the ceiling was sculptured, and showed it to her husband. Four years and nine months later, they found a ceiling similar to the one sketched by Mrs Hellström in an old royal palace in Cairo. An unusual feature of the ceiling was that the design had diagonal lines with flowers at the point of intersection of the lines. Mrs Hellström commented: 'All these years when we have travelled we have been looking for my ceiling. In Rome there are lots of similar ones, but they are never on the diagonal like this one. And also they have a flower in the middle of the square and not at the point of intersection.' The ceiling 'seen' by Mrs Hellström had a medallion in the centre, as did the one in the palace in Cairo.

Mrs Hellström noted in her diary on 14 January 1951, that the ceiling in her vision had a 'pale yellow ground, possibly with gold and white stripes, sculptured.' Her diary for 16 October 1955, said that the ceiling in the Cairo palace, which was photographed by Dr Hellström, was 'in white and gold and yellow, very beautiful' and was also richly sculptured.

It may be argued, of course, that if Dr and Mrs Hellström searched in many countries they would be bound in time to find a ceiling which resembled the one 'seen' in the vision, but the fact remains that they both travelled widely and had not come across one before the visit to Cairo nor had they come across one similar to it after that. It is also worth noting that the ceiling was found in a palace which was not open to the public – Dr Hellström was in Egypt on official business – and that, according to Mrs Hellström, 'all the other ceilings in the palace were just painted, not sculptured, in tasteless designs and colours.'

Half of Mrs Hellström's precognitive experiences concerned

deaths, illnesses, accidents and disasters. Many of her other experiences concerned, as might be expected, rather trivial events: as I have indicated in my introduction, precognition of events is not confined to those that are dramatic or meaningful. An example is given in her diary for 29 December 1953:

> Had a nap and woke up and saw a number of peculiar faces around me. They looked like masks of devils and strange beings. I said aloud: 'No, I don't believe in such beings.' Then they disappeared. The day after, Bo and I went to the opera. In the interval we went down into the basement where objects from the dramatic museum were temporarily exhibited, dresses, etc. There was a stand with a lot of masks which were identical with my 'devils'. It was really comical.

During some of her experiences, not necessarily precognitive, Mrs Hellström felt what she called 'psychical fatigue' which hurt her around the thyroid gland. Readers of my book *The Unexplained* will remember that in the chapter on strange happenings in the park at Versailles, it is described how the Crooke family twice saw in 1908 the figure of a 'sketching lady.' The second time they saw the figure some of the party wished to stay longer but Mr Crooke, a painter was overcome with 'such terrible fatigue' that they all went home. Possibly the fatigue was similar to that felt by Mrs Hellström. It is also worth recalling that in the famous Cheltenham haunting case, Rose Despard felt conscious of a feeling of loss as if she had lost power to the figure of the tall woman in black. Other examples of this feeling of loss, or fatigue, could be given.

It will have been noted that quite frequently Mrs Hellström experienced her visions during an attack of migraine. Mr Alan Hencher, whose experiences are described in chapter ten on the work of the British Premonitions Bureau, is also subject to migraine. I referred this point to Dr Arthur Guirdham, a consultant psychiatrist and author, and he replied: 'There is certainly a connection in some cases between extra-sensory perception and migraine but it should be made very clear that this does not apply to all cases of migraine because (a) the latter is a very common condition and (b) different people have different definitions of what migraine means. Attacks of migraine in people so disposed can be precipitated by extra-sensory perception of a telepathic nature.'

Mrs Hellström said that in 1948-9 she tried some card guessing experiments with quite good results but she was usually alone and had not kept the records as they had no value. She had tried crystal gazing, table turning and automatic writing but without any success. While I was compiling this chapter I was in touch with Mrs Hellström. She pointed out that the cases decreased in number as she grew older. I am grateful to her for her help. It is unusual to have the opportunity of studying material compiled by someone who is so aware of the pitfalls in psychical research and who has taken such care with the evidential aspects of her cases.[1]

[1] A scientific study of Mrs Hellström's psychic experiences will be published soon. The author is Dr Rolf Ejvegaard who teaches psychology and philosophy in Stockholm.

2 A coming new world order?

Early in the morning of 31 January 1915, Dame Edith Lyttelton, a member of a well-known political and cricketing family and a writer, was sitting with a pencil in her hand at Hackwood (the home of Lord Curzon), near Basingstoke, Hampshire, in the dreamy, half-awake state in which automatic writing is usually produced. It was during the time of the first world war, that war to end all wars, and with the bitter awareness of the carnage that was taking place on the Western Front no one imagined that a second world war could take place only twenty years after the ending of hostilities. But presently her pencil moved without conscious volition over the paper in front of her.

'In the morning we are aware of the coming day,' the message started, giving, I believe, an indication that what followed was to be regarded as a glimpse of the future. It ended:

> The nemesis of Fate nearer and nearer – No respite now nearer much than you think and once it begins there is no stay – no one knows – the leaves of the autumn – they will fall in quiet – the fugitive armies – the overshadowing of fear the price of peace.
> *Nolens Volens*.[1]
> The Munich bond remember that – you will see strange things.

At that time references to the Munich bond meant nothing to the statesmen and generals controlling the course of the first world war and certainly nothing to Dame Edith, who was later to become a delegate to the League of Nations. But it is now generally accepted that the Treaty of Munich, signed by the British Prime Minister, Neville Chamberlain, and Hitler on 30

[1] Willy-nilly.

September 1938 postponed but did not avert the outbreak of the second world war; indeed, in the opinion of many, the Treaty, by allowing for the dismemberment of Czechoslovakia, made war inevitable. However, the Treaty was the price of a peace that lasted only one year and the signing of the document was certainly overshadowed by the fear of war.

Another script by Dame Edith possibly relating to the second world war was produced at 3 p.m. on 24 May 1915 at Falconhurst, Kent. It read:

> In the western fields carnage – marching – the vines on the hills, the vintage – flight – now mark this – behind the curtains of blackness there is light never doubt it – be of good cheer. The hand stretched out to stay Bechtesgaden – Markovitch.

The automatic scripts of Dame Edith, who died in 1948 at the age of eighty-three, are dealt with by me in detail in the opening chapter of *Frontiers of the Unknown*. Some scripts seemed to show knowledge of future events in the first world war, such as the sinking of the *Lusitania* (two scripts with references to the *Lusitania* were produced by Dame Edith before the outbreak of war and one contains the phrase 'foam and fire' which suggests a disaster); others contained references to the bombing of London. Some of the scripts are not as clear as they might be – for example, we do not know who Markovitch is, and Berchtesgaden, Hitler's mountain retreat, is misspelt – but anyone who has studied Dame Edith's scripts must be struck by the number of 'hits' in them when related to events in the future of which she could not have had conscious knowledge.

One of Dame Edith's friends was Mrs Zoë Richmond, an honorary associate of the SPR, who is author of *Evidence of Purpose* (Bell, 1938). Dame Edith's scripts were left to Mrs Richmond in her will and I have had the opportunity of studying many of them with her in her home at Dunmow, Essex.

In *Frontiers of the Unknown* I point out that the theme of a coming conflict continued in Dame Edith's scripts between the wars, and this certainly was a far from popular viewpoint. At times Dame Edith spoke in a state of slight dissociation, and the following words by her were taken down in her home in Great College Street, Westminster, at 10 p.m. on 2 March 1932 by Mrs Richmond:

The four horsemen in the East, do not think the efforts have all been in vain. Every thought every prayer helps – even those you think foolish and which may be foolish. But the vibrations of war are too strong to pierce, you can only work through those who are outside, but we say again – every thought every prayer helps. This thing is the beginning of a terrific struggle that will take many unforeseen shapes. In a sense the whole world will be involved. . . .

I see a very curious looking instrument. At first I thought it was a miniature machine gun, but I think it is a very sharply pointed sort of telescope mounted on a sort of little carriage wheels and it has a great force – it is called 'the pencil of light.' It is manipulated from far away. I don't know what it means. . . .

This particular script had not been published before. The phrase 'the pencil of light' at once brought to mind a laser beam. The word laser stands for 'light amplification by stimulated emission of radiation'. An article headed 'Laser – the Light Fantastic' in the *Reader's Digest* of May 1967 described the laser as 'the marvellous new device that shoots out narrow, highly concentrated beams of light – the sharpest, purest, most intense light ever known.' Although a great deal had been written about the laser's potentialities as a death ray, inquiries I made at the Ministry of Defence and in other circles in London in 1967, when I was revising *Frontiers of the Unknown*, brought little information of a practical nature except that lasers could be used for range-finding.

However, by 1973 the position had altered. A Defence Ministry spokesman said: 'I can confirm that work on the use of laser beams as destructive weapons has been in progress for the Navy, RAF, and the Army for some time. We also have a close exchange of information with the US on this subject, which is highly classified.'

Articles in the Press said that millions of pounds were being spent on developing 'death-ray weapons' for destroying planes, missiles and tanks. Mr Chapman Pincher said in the London *Daily Express* that 'the ray which is making science fiction into reality is a laser light beam boosted to such power it can punch holes in metal at long range.'

He added that the laser beam, which can be generated in various ways, travels with the speed of light so a laser gun has plenty of time to pick up an incoming missile and could be made powerful enough to destroy it at a height of seventy miles. Fitted to aircraft, laser guns would be more devastating than any anti-aircraft missile because of their speed and range. Mobile laser ray machines on the battlefield could shoot down attacking aircraft by igniting the fuel tanks or even killing the pilots.

A report from Robin Smyth in Washington in the *Daily Mail* of 31 January 1973 said that President Nixon had ordered an all-out effort to develop the laser bomb – a hydrogen bomb triggered by an intensely concentrated ray of light. He had set aside £14,000,000 in his new budget for the development of the bomb during the coming year. This was more than half the Atomic Energy Commission's total budget for weapons research. The light beam, which generates intense heat, allows for a much smaller bomb which can be fitted more easily into the warhead of an intercontinental ballistic missile. Russia was also known to be working on a laser bomb.

The first paper describing how a laser might be made was published in the December 1958 issue of the *Physical Review* by Dr C. H. Townes and his brother-in-law, Dr Arthur Schawlow. At that time Townes was a professor at Columbia University, and Schawlow was at the nearby Bell Telephone Laboratories at Murray Hill, New Jersey. The first beam was emitted in the United States in 1960.

When we examine some of the statements made by journalists about the military uses of devices employing laser beams we are struck by the number of 'hits' in Dame Edith's script. She 'saw' what she first thought was a weapon and then thought was 'a very sharply pointed sort of telescope mounted on a sort of little carriage wheels.' This suggests that the instrument (or weapon) is mobile. Mr Chapman Pincher, it will be remembered, referred to mobile laser ray machines which could shoot down attacking aircraft. Dame Edith said that the object she saw 'has a great force'. We know that laser beams have a great force. The 'pencil of light', Dame Edith said, 'is manipulated from far away.' If laser beams were used to trigger atomic bombs the operation would obviously have to be carried out a considerable distance from the bomb.

The key phrase in the script is 'the pencil of light' and the laser beam is precisely that. Dame Edith described what she 'saw' in her vision, made certain statements (mobility, force, manipulated from far away), and ended by saying: 'I don't know what it means.'

The laser at that time (1932) was not even a concept in the minds of men. Mr Chapman Pincher ended his article in the *Daily Express* of 22 May 1973 by stating that 'secret work in Britain and the US has now shown that death ray weapons are almost certainly feasible and could be in service in the next decade.'

If this should be so, some may conclude that Dame Edith's script contained a prediction about the practical application on the battlefield of a beam which was not to be emitted until nearly thirty years later.

Dame Edith was one of about a dozen automatists, all, except one, members of the SPR, who took part in the cross-correspondences which, in the opinion of some eminent psychical researchers, have provided the most convincing evidence yet of intelligent communication from beyond the grave.

From 1901 onwards references in scripts had appeared with a persistence which seemed to indicate that they came from a number of communicators who were dead. There were seven of them and they included Professor Henry Sidgwick, the first President of the SPR, F. W. H. Myers, poet and classical scholar, who died in 1901, and Edmund Gurney, principal author of *Phantasms of the Living*, one of the classics of psychical research, who died in 1888. They may seem like figures of a bygone age to many modern readers, but some of the material in the scripts, amounting to 3,000 documents and taken down over a period of thirty years, is relevant to the present day and to the unfolding future.

The scripts, some in Latin and Greek and all with literary and classical allusions, were sent to a small group of interpreters who discovered that, although a script might be meaningless by itself, it made sense when compared with a script submitted by another automatist.

What is the message of the scripts in this famous experiment?

For a long time it was regarded as an effort to provide proof of the survival of the communicators, but in 1950 Mr J. G. Piddington, one of the interpreters of the scripts, said that they clearly predicted a new era of peace among nations and classes. This view was confirmed independently by Mr W. H. Salter in his book *Zoar* to which I have already made reference.

Little attention has been paid to these conclusions by Piddington and Salter and that is why I am including them in a book on precognition.

It is virtually impossible, within the confines of one chapter, to give a summary of the cross-correspondences which occupy nearly 3,000 pages of the *Proceedings* of the SPR, particularly as an education in the classics is essential for the understanding of them.

A number of the scripts concerned ancient Rome. Salter points out that in several of his writings Myers takes the story of Rome as told in the *Aeneid* of Virgil as symbolic of the spiritual evolution of mankind, 'a labour continuing through all the ages.' When, however, Mrs A. W. Verrall, one of the more noted of the automatists and a classical scholar, quotes the *Aeneid* in her scripts, as she often does, it is to illustrate a different ideal, not a process of gradual evolution over an indefinite period of time, but a practical policy to be worked for in her own age, an international order embodying all that was best in the *Pax Augusta.*

Salter states in *Zoar*: 'As declared in the scripts, the ultimate purpose of the Communicators, or of the script intelligence if that phrase is preferred, was the bringing about of a world order based on international peace and social justice. This is not a trivial project nor one unworthy of the persons represented as engaging in it.'

No precise date was assigned to the completion of this ultimate aim but the beginning, at least, was within the lifetime of persons living at the time of the first world war.

Mr Colin Brookes-Smith, in a paper on 'A Humanist Reaction to SPR Literature' in the SPR *Journal* of June 1963, speculates on the possible fulfilment of prophecy in the scripts on the coming world order. It should be noted, he said, that by 1920 a considerable start had been made in England on special measures which, by the ultimate creation of the welfare state, had produced greater equality and therefore peace between classes. It was a matter of opinion whether this could in any way be taken as a fulfilment of one part of the prediction. Nevertheless, we should not lose sight of the fact that despite the second world war and the subsequent phase of nuclear rearmament, there did seem to be a growing realization that the possession of means of total destruction was self-defeating. The more nuclear missiles there were, the more anxious political leaders seemed to be that none should be fired.

However, there are dissenting views of the value of the cross-correspondences.

Dr Thouless, in *From Anecdote to Experiment in Psychical Research*, says that if this (the cross-correspondences) was an experiment devised by these scholars on the other side of the grave, it must be judged to be a badly designed experiment. It had provided a mass of material of which it was very difficult to judge the evidential value and about which there were varying opinions. It reproduced, in fact, the defects of spontaneously gathered mediumistic material in a somewhat intensified form. A successful experiment should give a more clear and unambiguous answer to the question it was designed to answer than did spontaneous material; otherwise the experiment was not worth while. When judged by this criterion the cross-correspondences would seem to fail as an experiment.

In a hitherto unpublished letter written to me in 1968 Professor C. D. Broad said: 'My own reaction to much of the cross-correspondences is decidedly chilly. If one has *not* steeped oneself in them, one is not in a position to judge for oneself; and, if one *has* done so, one is in the danger of getting into the state of a Bacon-Shakespeare enthusiast.' He went on to ask: 'Have you ever read Ronald Knox's very ingenious, detailed "spoof" that *In Memoriam* was written by Queen Victoria who left covert indications, in the poetry, of her authorship?'

I have considerable sympathy for the views of Dr Thouless and Dr Broad. Much of the material is ambiguous and difficult to follow. A great deal of the matter in the scripts is so complex that one cannot say without fear of contradiction from people of clear and analytical mind who have given the scripts deep study that the evidence for a design by a mind or minds behind the scripts is there for all to see. It plainly is not. Yet, on the other hand, there is in the cross-correspondences evidence of something very strange in operation over a long period. For instance, 'Mrs Holland' (the pseudonym given to Alice Kipling, sister of Rudyard Kipling) was directed by her script to write to Mrs Verrall at an address in Cambridge. Some of the scripts were signed by the ostensible communicators, who gave specific directions to the automatists and commented on the success or otherwise of the experiment.

On 13 July 1904, Mr Piddington wrote a 'posthumous' letter at the SPR offices in London, sealed it and gave it to Miss Johnson, the secretary, to keep. The letter began: 'If ever I am a spirit, and if I can communicate, I shall endeavour to remember to transmit in some form or other the number SEVEN. . . .

During the next few years some of the automatists produced scripts containing references to seven people or objects (the seven-branched candlestick and the seven colours of the rainbow are examples occurring in one script, that of Mrs Verrall, written on 11 May 1908).

Mrs Verrall did not even know that Piddington's 'posthumous' message existed. On 27 January 1909, she wrote a 'Myers' script ending with the following passage:

> And ask what has been the success of Piddington's last experiment? Has he found the bits of his famous sentence scattered among you all? And does he think that is accident, or started by one of you? But even if the source is human, who carries the thoughts to the receivers? Ask him that. F.W.H.M.

The 'sevens' experiment provides, at the very least, evidence for telepathy and possibly something even more significant.

We should now ask ourselves whether there is any sign of the birth of a new world order as predicted, according to Piddington and Salter, in the scripts.

Whatever view we take of the cross-correspondences, it cannot be denied that seventy years on from the time when the scripts started, shortly after the turn of the century, we are living in a vastly different world from the one that prevailed then. The first world war started a process of change that was continued by the second and shows no sign of losing its momentum. Countries in Europe have had their boundaries changed and, even more significant, huge territories in Africa and Asia that were under colonial domination are now independent. Something very strange is going on in the world of science. Those who wish to follow up this matter, particularly in respect of quantum theory, may do so in Mr Arthur Koestler's *The Roots of Coincidence* (Random House, 1972). The laws of mechanics, so Sir Arthur Eddington assures us in *The Nature of the Physical World* (The University of Michigan Press, 1958), 'have lost their halo; only the popular writer still thinks them sacrosanct'.

A generation that has never known world war is now growing up and is seeking self-expression in many directions, not all of them praiseworthy. Churches that had clung with grim determination to their orthodoxies now find their priests deserting them in droves. The other side of the coin is a manifestation of the religious impulse in man which is finding expression through various outlets: I do not think it is an exaggeration to say that the Church is being reborn. Although there has been conflict in the Middle East and the Far East, the great power blocs have avoided direct involvement. If another world war started, a great many young people, I believe, would not give it their active and continued support. It is only necessary to look back to the first world war, with the rush of volunteers and the idealism of poets such as Rupert Brooke, to see how popular attitudes to war have changed.

Those who doubt that we are indeed entering a new world era have only to turn to a book by Alvin Toffler, *Future Shock* (Random House, 1970), to learn the extent of the change. 'Change,' says Toffler, 'is avalanching upon our heads and most people are grotesquely unprepared to cope with it.' He then asks:

> Is all this exaggerated? I think not. It has become a cliché to say that what we are now living through is 'a second industrial revolution.' This phrase is supposed to impress us with the speed and profundity of the change around us. But in addition to being platitudinous, it is misleading. For what is occurring now is, in all likelihood, bigger, deeper and more important than the industrial revolution. Indeed, a growing body of reputable opinion asserts that the present moment represents nothing less than the second great divide in human history, comparable in magnitude only with that first break in historic continuity, the shift from barbarism to civilization.

Mr Toffler emphasized this viewpoint in an article in *The Observer* of 31 December 1972, in which he said:

> What we detect in the air is nothing less than the smell of decay that accompanies the end of an era. And, indeed, I would argue that we are all – Americans, Britons, Japanese, Swedes, Germans, Italians and Frenchmen alike – up against a fundamental revolution so deep, so unprecedented, and so potentially violent, that it dwarfs all previous revolutions in human history.

What Mr Toffler and others are writing now does seem to have been anticipated in the scripts of the cross-correspondences, if we accept Mr Piddington's and Mr Salter's interpretation of them. But whether the new world order will be based on international peace and social justice is quite another matter.

I started this chapter with Dame Edith Lyttelton's predictions of the second world war and will end with predictions which point to a war still to come. These predictions were given for the first time in *Frontiers of the Unknown.*

In this chapter, I pointed out that many will remember that the first world war was regarded as a war to end wars. Dame Edith, as a delegate to the League of Nations Assembly, could be expected to understand fully this view, but the theme of coming conflict and order emerging out of chaos, continued in her scripts *after* the ending of the war. This, some will think, suggests that she was guided by intelligences which knew that the break in hostilities was only a temporary one.

What of the future, and prophecies in the scripts that are as yet unfulfilled? Mrs Richmond, who keeps Dame Edith's unpublished war scripts in a book, made a note in January 1955 to this effect:

> For years now I have regarded these scripts as referring to three wars, the two that have passed, and the one to come; and they treat the whole period as one to my mind.
>
> A period of rebirth for the world and humanity, involving the inevitable destruction that such a rebirth must involve.
>
> Yet all the time we are urged to have faith in the ultimate victory of spiritual values, which are assured.

The two relevant scripts follow. It must be remembered that, as products of impressions received in the subconscious, they will contain some material which is ambiguous and seemingly irrelevant.

17 January 1924, Fishers Hill (Woking), 12.20 a.m.
. . . something about victory . . . the golden opportunity once, twice and the third the greatest. Boanerges and the lightning – the scotched snakes (*long pause*) the flight in winter – Nelson, Nelson's column – it will serve the watchword – a dictator.

29 March 1924, 11.15 p.m., Old Rosery (Reigate)
. . . Toy tents on grass the spring of the year – comes the great up-

heaval, courage he said and pointed to the dawn . . . the morning star cast is thy lot – Miltonic dialogue lest any fail.

There is much here that is vague, but the script of 29 March 1924 suggests that a great war will start in the spring. The first and second world wars started in the autumn.

3 The sinking of the *Titanic*

On 10 April 1912, Mr and Mrs Jack Marshall and their family were on the roof of their home overlooking the Solent opposite the Isle of Wight watching the progress of the White Star liner *Titanic*, the largest ship in the world, which had sailed that day from Southampton on her maiden voyage to New York. Mrs Marshall suddenly clutched her husband's arm and cried out, 'That ship is going to sink before she reaches America.'

Her husband tried to soothe her, but her agitation only increased. Others present tried to persuade Mrs Marshall that the *Titanic* had been built in a new way which made it impossible for her to sink. At this she only became angry and said, 'Don't stand there staring at me! Do something! You fools, I can see hundreds of people struggling in the icy water! Are you all so blind that you are going to let them drown?'

Among those present was Mrs Marshall's daughter, Joan Grant, who relates this incident in her autobiography *Far Memory* (Harper, New York, 1956). She said, 'During the next five days everyone was careful not to mention the *Titanic*, but Mother was nervy and Father looked harassed. It must have been almost a relief for her when everyone knew that the *Titanic* had struck an iceberg; not nearly so lonely as waiting until it happened.'

The *Titanic*, 882.5 feet long and weighing 46,328 gross tons, had, for those days, the extraordinary speed of twenty-four to twenty-five knots. She had a double bottom and fifteen watertight bulkheads which could be closed almost instantly to seal off compartments of the ship. Unfortunately, these bulkheads extended only partway up the hull. The builders had announced that the vessel was unsinkable, and the scientific and lay public believed them. This belief was shared by the 2,207 passengers and crew on board. On 14 April, Captain Smith, the *Titanic*'s master, received five warnings of icebergs in the vicinity of the ship. These made him uneasy but not enough to slow down the ship, although all other ships in the area had slowed down or stopped altogether. At 11.40 p.m. that night, under full speed, she struck an iceberg which ripped a gash in five of her forward watertight compartments. Water rapidly rushed into the damaged front compartments and tipped the bow down so that it then ran over the top of the fifth bulkhead and flowed into the next compartment, and so on. The ship did not capsize but tilted down so that the stern gradually rose while the bow sank, and it finally slid into the water at a steep angle.

The *Titanic* sank at 2.20 a.m. on 15 April. She carried far too few lifeboats and many of these were not filled when they were lowered and rowed away. About 1,502 people lost their lives, the estimates varying slightly in different reports.

Mrs Marshall was not alone in fearing for the safety of the passengers and crew of the *Titanic*, despite the general conviction of the ship's unsinkability. Mr J. Connon Middleton, an English businessman, booked a passage in the *Titanic* on 23 March. About a week later, i.e. ten days before the sailing date, he dreamt that he saw her 'floating on the sea, keel upwards, and her passengers and crew swimming around her.'

The following night he experienced the same dream. These dreams made him 'uncomfortable', and he was subsequently 'most depressed and even despondent'.

Mr Middleton did not cancel his passage until about four days after the first dream. He did so then because he had received a cable from the United States telling him that for business reasons he should postpone his sailing for a few days. After he had cancelled his ticket, Mr Middleton told members of his family and friends about his dream, prior to the actual sailing and sinking of the ship (it is worth noting, however, that the details of the manner of sinking of the ship in the dream were incorrect). Mr Middleton's listeners subsequently testified that he had done this. Two of the persons to whom Mr Middleton had told his dreams mentioned in their reports, published in the *Proceedings* of the SPR, vol. 15 (1912), that in his dream he himself 'seemed to be floating in the air just above the wreck.'

Mrs Middleton stated that her husband 'never dreams' and had certainly never had a dream of this kind before.

On Wednesday, 10 April (the day the *Titanic* sailed), a sensitive, Mr V. N. Turvey, predicted that 'a great liner will be lost.' On Saturday, 13 April, he communicated this prediction in a letter to a Madame I. de Steiger, with the further statement that the liner would be lost in two days. Madame de Steiger received the letter on the following Monday, 15 April.[1]

Among the passengers who lost their lives in the sinking was W. T. Stead, the distinguished journalist and editor, and a prominent Spiritualist. He seems to have had an inkling of his fate in a number of curious ways. In the 1880s, when he was editor of the *Pall Mall Gazette*, he published a fictional article in the form of a survivor's tale of the sinking of a great liner. The article 'showed how the majority of the passengers were doomed beforehand.' Stead added an editorial note: 'This is exactly what might take place, and what will take place, if liners are sent to sea short of boats.'

In 1892, Stead published another article in the *Review of Reviews*, in which he pictured the sinking of a liner by collision with an iceberg and the rescue of its sole surviving passenger by a White Star liner, the *Majestic*. The captain of the real *Majestic* of that time was Captain Smith, who subsequently became captain of the *Titanic* and lost his life in the sinking.

Pertaining more specifically to himself, Stead later described a 'vision' as follows: 'I had a vision of a mob, and this had made me feel that I shall not die in a way common to the most of us, but by violence, and one of many in a throng.' Stead only mentioned this premonition, however, after a mob had handled him roughly, because of his pacifist views, during the riotous celebration in London of the relief of Mafeking in 1900.

In 1909 Stead gave a lecture to the Cosmos Club in which he pictured himself as shipwrecked and calling for help.

Count Harmon, a sensitive whom Stead consulted from time to time, told him that danger to his life 'would be from water, and from nothing else'. On 21 June 1911, this sensitive advised

[1] This correspondence was published in *Light*, the magazine of what is now the College of Psychic Studies, London, in June, 1912.

Stead in a letter that 'travel would be dangerous to him in the month of April, 1912.'

Another sensitive, Mr W. de Kerlor, consulted by Stead, made several statements about his future over a period of some months beginning in September, 1911. In the first interview Mr de Kerlor predicted that Stead would go to America, although he had no such plans or wishes at the time. Among other things the sensitive said:

> I can see . . . the picture of a huge black ship, of which I see the back portion; where the name of the ship should be written there is a wreath of immortelles . . . I can only see half of the ship: that symbol may mean by the time the ship will be completed – when one will be able to see it in its whole length, it is perhaps then that you will go on your journey.

Later the sensitive had a dream which he related to Mr Stead as applying to him. He said, 'I dreamt that I was in the midst of a catastrophe in the water; there were masses (more than a thousand) of bodies struggling in the water and I was among them. I could hear their cries for help.'

Mr de Kerlor told this dream to Mr Stead and repeated also his warning that the black ship, of the previous precognition, 'meant limitations, difficulties and death'. These prognostications did not influence Stead, who replied, 'Oh, yes; well, well, you are a very gloomy prophet.'

A few hours before the ship struck the iceberg, one of the first-class passengers, Mr Charles M. Hays, President of the Grand Trunk Railroad, said that the time would soon come for 'the greatest and most appalling of all disasters at sea'. Later that night, a little after the ship had struck the iceberg and was listing slightly, Mr Hays remained unconcerned and said, 'You cannot sink this boat.' At 12.45 a.m., with the bow already quite low and after the crew had begun to load and lower the lifeboats, Hays remarked, 'This ship is good for eight hours yet.' It sank one and a half hours later.

The above cases are taken from a review and analysis of paranormal experiences connected with the sinking of the *Titanic* by Professor Ian Stevenson, MD, in the *Journal* of the American Society for Psychical Research for October 1960. Dr Stevenson, who holds the chair of Parapsychology at the University of

Virginia, lists twelve seemingly paranormal experiences but only some of these are precognitive.

In the *Journal* of the American SPR for July 1965, Dr Stevenson gives seven more paranormal experiences associated with the sinking of the *Titanic*.

One concerned Mr Colin Macdonald, who in 1912 was a thirty-three-years-old marine engineer already with considerable experience in ships crossing the Atlantic. When the *Titanic*'s crew was being selected he was offered the position of second engineer. This would have meant an important promotion for such a young engineer, but Mr Macdonald had a 'hunch' that he should not sail in the *Titanic*. The offer of the post in the *Titanic* was made three times altogether, but Mr Macdonald repeatedly declined it. The man who took the place he turned down as second engineer, Mr J. Hesketh, lost his life in the disaster.

Dr Stevenson learned of this case through reading an obituary notice of Mr Macdonald in a newspaper. He saw the dead man's daughter, Mrs Isabel Fernsworth, on 10 October 1964, and she narrated to him what her father had told her of his experience. She also showed him a newspaper account of an interview with her father published about four years before this. Mrs Fernsworth stated that her father corrected a mistake in the newspaper account and that it then accorded with what he remembered of the experience and had often narrated to his family or other persons.

Mrs Norah K. Mathews sent Dr Stevenson a written account, together with a covering letter dated 30 October 1964, of a scene that took place when she heard that her mother, a stewardess, was to sail in the *Titanic*.

I was about eleven years of age when I first heard that my mother, Mrs Mary Keziah Roberts . . . was going to sail in the great new ship called the *Titanic* (said Mrs Mathews). I was a very reserved and quiet child, but very deeply impressed.

I looked at my dear mother, who was gaily combing her . . . hair. She was looking at me in the looking glass for a few minutes . . . and I looked at her and she smiled and threw her head back and sang; she had a sweet musical voice too. She sang 'Yip-i-addie-i-aye . . . I don't care what becomes of me . . . lah, lah, lah. . . .' Then I turned to her and said quietly, 'Mama, why do you sing like that?' I felt sad and could not say very much. I said again, 'I don't want you to sing that song again; I don't want you to sail in the *Titanic*.' With this she stopped combing her lovely long hair, and stopped singing and stopped laughing too. After a few minutes she said to me whilst still looking into the looking glass at me, 'Oh, Tabby, Tabby, I must tell your father about that'. She was going to sing again . . . then just went on combing her hair and I looked through the window quietly, with a strange sense of doom. Certainly no elation. We were living at 9 Chestnut Grove, West Bridgford, Nottingham, at the time. My father, David Roberts, became quite impressed at what I had said, as I was nine years of age when I first had most powerful and correct impressions.

In answer to an inquiry from Dr Stevenson, Mrs Mathews wrote that she thought that 'something was going to happen both to my mother and also to the fine new boat she was going shortly to sail on'. Mrs Mathews also placed her impression as occurring 'very close' to the time the *Titanic* sailed, but she could not give a precise interval in terms of days or weeks.

Mrs Roberts, who was in the official crew list of the *Titanic* as a stewardess, survived the sinking.

Mrs Mathews also sent Dr Stevenson accounts of several other impressions or visual images she experienced when some misfortune was about to happen or was happening to a member of the family. Among these examples was another occasion (about 1916) when she tried to prevent her mother from sailing in a hospital ship, the *Rohilla*. The ship sank and Mrs Roberts, who disregarded her daughter's warning, again escaped.

As Mr and Mrs Roberts are dead, Dr Stevenson was unable to obtain confirmation of the warnings given by Mrs Mathews as a child.

Another English girl who had a strange experience connected with the sinking of the *Titanic* is now Mrs Hughes, of 19a Shelton Old Road, Stoke-on-Trent. She gave an account of it in a letter of July 1963 to Dr Stevenson and he interviewed her the following month.

The most vivid dream I ever had (said Mrs Hughes) was when I was fourteen. I was on the main road at Hanford which was then Trentham Road and now it's Stone Road when suddenly I saw a very large ship a short distance away as if in Trentham Park. I saw figures walking about and I just stood wondering what it was doing there. Suddenly it lowered at one end and I heard a terrific scream. I must have woke up making a noise because I frightened Gran. She said, 'No more suppers for you, lady; dreams are a pack of daft,' after I had told her what I'd seen.

After a while I must have gone to sleep again and saw the very same scene and when the people screamed I must have done. Gran was real livid with me this time and said I wasn't stopping with her again at night.

This all happened on the Friday night 12 April 1912. The next morning I told my mother and I was really very upset at what I'd seen and what Gran had said.

It transpired later that Mrs Hughes's uncle, Mr Leonard Hodgkinson, senior fourth engineer in the *Titanic*, had lost his life in the sinking. Trentham Gardens adjoining the Park contained a large lake, with facilities for boating, and Dr Stevenson comments in his study that 'the map of the area shows that from the position the dreamer seemed to be in (on the Stone Road at Hanford looking south towards Trentham Park) the large lake in the adjoining Trentham Gardens would be included in the field of vision so that a boat in the lake might well seem to be "as if in Trentham Park" '.

As Mrs Hughes's mother and grandmother had died, it was impossible for Dr Stevenson to obtain confirmation of her account.

Among the nineteen apparently paranormal experiences associated with the sinking of the *Titanic* listed by Professor Stevenson in his two papers, were a number of dreams which occurred on the night of the sinking. Some of these were startlingly accurate.

A woman in New York awoke from a vivid dream during the night of the sinking and awakened her husband to tell him about it. 'I just saw Mother in a crowded lifeboat rocking in the ocean swell. The boat was so crowded with people that it looked as if it might be swamped any minute.' The dreamer countered her husband's scoffing by firm statements that 'this wasn't just a bad dream – it was – well, it was different. It was something so awful – frightening, and all so real.' When the newspapers published the story of the sinking of the *Titanic* the dreamer discovered with horror the name of her mother in the passenger list. Her mother survived the sinking and reached New York safely. According to Mr W. O. Stevens, who relates this incident in *The Mystery of Dreams* (Dodd, Mead and Co., New York, 1949):

The mother told her daughter that she had taken passage in the *Titanic* without letting her know because she wanted to surprise her. And at the very time when the daughter had that dream of her mother wallowing on a dark sea, that was precisely her situation. She said that she expected momentarily that the boat would capsize, and all the while her thoughts were concentrated on the daughter, whom she never expected to see again.

However, this was not a precognitive dream.

Professor Stevenson includes in his list of apparently paranormal experiences accompanying the sinking of the *Titanic* the novel which seemed to foretell the fate of the great liner.

In 1898, a writer named Morgan Robertson wrote a novel called *Futility* in which he described the building and an early voyage of a huge steamship which he named the *Titan*. On this voyage, in April, the ship sank after a collision with an iceberg. The *Titan* also was believed unsinkable by virtue of having water-tight compartments. She also carried too few lifeboats and consequently her sinking resulted in an appalling loss of life.

Other details of the *Titan* and its sinking resembled those of the *Titanic*, viz.:

	Titan	*Titanic*
Number of persons aboard	3,000	2,207
Number of lifeboats	24	20
Speed at impact with iceberg	25 knots	23 knots
Displacement tonnage of the liner	75,000	66,000
Length of the liner	800 feet	882.5 feet
Number of propellers	3	3

Dr Stevenson comments: 'I think we can consider the correspondence either exact or impressive on the following ten points: name of ship; myth of unsinkability; collision with iceberg; sinking in month of April; displacement tonnage; length of ship; speed of ship at impact; number of propellers; enormous loss of life.'

In the course of discussion of various aspects of cases outlined here, Dr Stevenson points out that we must distinguish between inference and apparent precognition. Morgan Robertson's novel is considered in this light.

At first glance, the ten points of correspondence (exact or near) between Robertson's *Titan* and the *Titanic* may strongly suggest precognition. However, we certainly cannot exclude inference as a source of

Robertson's story. At the end of the nineteenth century confidence in engineering skill ran high with few limits to its achievement discernible. The novels of Jules Verne and H. G. Wells predicted further extraordinary developments. That science has outrun science fiction we all know. But we also know that the advance of engineering proceeds jerkily, the reach of science from time to time exceeding its grasp. Unanticipated obstacles arise, and these often bring disaster before new tactics finally master them. . . . A writer of the 1890s familiar with man's repeated *hubris* might reasonably infer that he would overreach himself in the construction of ocean liners which then, with skyscrapers and airplanes just beginning, were man's greatest engineering marvels. Granting then, a penetrating awareness of man's growing and excessive confidence in marine engineering, a thoughtful person might make additional inferences about the details of the tragedy to come. A large ship would probably have great power and speed; the name *Titan* has connoted power and security for several thousand years; overconfidence would neglect the importance of lifeboats; recklessness would race the ship through the areas of the Atlantic icebergs; these drift south in the spring, making April a likely month for collision.

In summary, I think one might infer that confidence would, for a time, suppress caution in the building and management of ocean liners. Robertson was not the only person to think this. W. T. Stead also seems to have imagined a marine disaster with an appalling loss of life resulting from inadequate numbers of lifeboats. Having reached the general conclusion of the probability of such a disaster, inferences, such as those I have suggested, might fill in details to provide correspondences which would have an appearance of precognition but which we should, I believe, consider only successful inferences.

However, says Dr Stevenson, this raises the limits we might put to the powers of inference before considering it reasonably excluded from cases in which we are also considering the possibility of precognition.

Mr G. W. Lambert is another who considers that inference, rather than precognition, accounts for the number of 'hits' in Robertson's novel. Robertson, he says in the *Journal* of the SPR, for June 1962, had studied form in the shipping world, and had a sound basis of knowledge from which to speculate about future developments. Features in his novel were nearly all deducible from the size of the vessel. Once he had successfully guessed the size of the ship, it was a matter of calculation, rather than prediction, to get 'right' or nearly 'right', the length, tonnage, numbers of passengers, lifeboats and propellers, and so on.

When we look back on the apparently paranormal experiences associated with the sinking of the *Titanic* we must remember that many people are fearful of what might happen on a voyage, whether by sea or by air. It is not unusual for people, acting on 'hunches', to cancel arrangements for a journey. Mr W. E. Cox published in the *Journal* of the American SPR for July 1956, the results of a study which showed that on days when a number of important railway accidents occurred most of the trains involved in the accidents carried fewer passengers than these same trains ordinarily did under comparable traffic conditions. He found significant differences between the number of passengers on the days of the accidents and on the days without accidents. Mr Cox suggested that some unconscious precognition of the forthcoming accident deterred passengers who had planned to travel from doing so on the days when accidents occurred. Cancellations are sometimes made for reasons which are not immediately obvious. For instance, a clerk of the White Star Line acknowledged that many persons had refused to sail in the *Titanic* because of a superstitious fear of maiden voyages.

However, we must also bear in mind that the usual fears for safety did not apply to the maiden voyage of the *Titanic* because the vessel was considered unsinkable; certainly Captain Smith must have thought so because he did not reduce speed, as he almost certainly would have done in another vessel, when icebergs were reported on his route. As Dr Stevenson points out, 'both crew and passengers firmly believed in the ship's unlimited buoyancy.' In these circumstances there should have been fewer premonitions of disaster than usual. Instead of this, Dr Stevenson, when he had totted up nineteen apparently paranormal experiences connected with the sinking, considered that 'this disaster clearly becomes the one most associated with reported extrasensory perceptions.'

The warnings of disaster varied from the vague to the specific. One of the first-class passengers, Miss Edith Evans, as the ship sank, recalled that a fortune-teller had once told her to 'beware of the water'. Miss Evans gave up her place in a lifeboat to another passenger and perished. Warnings about danger from water are part of the stock-in-trade of fortune-tellers and there is no indication from the information available to us that the warning given to Miss Evans applied to the voyage of the *Titanic*. On the other hand, Mrs Marshall became distressed as she watched the great liner set out on her maiden voyage and, from what was obviously a visionary experience, described to her surprised family a scene of 'hundreds of people struggling in the icy water'. This prediction was fulfilled five days later.

Mr Middleton's personal warning came in a dream but it was one he disregarded until he received a cable from the United States telling him that for business reasons he should postpone his sailing for a few days. Mrs Middleton testified that her husband had said 'how foolish it would seem if he postponed his business on account of a dream.' If the cable from New York had not arrived he would presumably have sailed in the *Titanic* and possibly perished.

Dr Stevenson discusses this point in his study and gives two other examples of how warnings about this disaster were not taken seriously:

> W. T. Stead received rather clear warnings (although to be sure not specifically mentioning the *Titanic*), but did not act on them. And we have seen that Mr Charles Hays predicted an appalling marine disaster, but a few hours later had the utmost difficulty in thinking that what he himself had said could apply to himself even though it was by then obvious to most persons aboard that the ship was sinking rapidly. These three persons (he includes Mr Middleton) then seem to have had, in varying degrees, warning experiences which they did not apply to themselves, or at least not sufficiently to take appropriate action.
>
> I include no reproach in this analysis of their behaviour. Most other persons would have acted no differently. Accurate precognitions occur too rarely (probably) to form a reasonable basis for action in everyday life. The records of apparent precognition contain numerous examples of experiences which induced action and also numerous examples which the percipients ignored (at least with regard to action) until after the events foretold had taken place. We should interest ourselves in the motives which separate those who act upon premonitions from those who do not. A cultural climate hostile to psychical experiences may influence percipients not to act on perceptions when a more favourable climate might encourage them to do so. (Because it is not otherwise relevant here, I will only mention the occurrence of the opposite extreme in primitive societies and in some

superstitious or mentally ill persons who act upon the vaguest hints or supposed premonitions).

In this chapter I have given ten examples of apparent precognition concerning the sinking of the *Titanic* or nine if we exclude Morgan Robertson's novel, as I feel we should. When we analyse them, we see that the information came to Mrs Marshall in a vision; Mr Middleton and Mrs Hughes had dreams; one sensitive, Mr de Kerlor, told Mr Stead that he could 'see . . . the picture of a huge black ship' and later he had a dream which he related to Mr Stead as applying to him; two other sensitives, Mr Turvey and Count Harmon, did not give details of the form of their experience; Mrs Mathews thought something was going to happen to her mother and the ship in which she was going to sail; and Mr Macdonald had a 'hunch' that he should not sail in the *Titanic*.

Mrs Hughes, Mrs Mathews and Mr Macdonald had had other extra-sensory experiences. There was some evidence (or claim) of additional extra-sensory experiences on the part of others mentioned in Dr Stevenson's study. He says: 'In short, we have some grounds for believing that of the nineteen percipients, at least twelve had other extra-sensory perceptions besides their experiences related to the *Titanic*. And since we lack much information, the true incidence may be higher.'

It must be remembered that the nineteen experiences given by Dr Stevenson were not all precognitive. One about which I had doubts related to the Reverend Charles Morgan, minister of the Rosedale Methodist Church in Winnipeg, Canada, who, on the evening of 14 April, drew up a list of hymns to be sung at the evening service of that church. He then relaxed on a couch and seemed to drift into a trancelike state in which he saw vividly presented to him the number of an unfamiliar hymn. He felt compelled to have that hymn sung at his service, although he did not recognize it from the number before calling it out for the congregation to sing. The hymn of this number turned out to be 'Hear, Father, while we pray to Thee, for those in peril on the sea.' At the time the congregation was singing this strangely selected hymn in Winnipeg, passengers in the second-class dining-room of the *Titanic* were also singing it at the request of the Reverend Ernest Carter, one of the second-class passengers. This occurred about two hours before the *Titanic* struck the iceberg. Dr Stevenson thinks the example given here is 'indicative of unconscious precognition'. Whether this is so is a matter of opinion.

Six of Dr Stevenson's examples of apparent precognition took place several months or longer before the sinking of the *Titanic* and four within ten days or fewer of the disaster.

Pointing out that in the Aberfan coal-tip disaster eighteen of thirty-four[2] precognitions occurred within four days of it, Dr Stevenson states:

> this piling up of precognitive experiences as the related events come nearer is, I think, harmonious with the suggestion . . . that the percipient subconsciously makes normal inferences from paranormally derived information. Presumably as an event comes nearer to actualization the causal processes that will bring it about become less subject to modification. The event becomes more inevitable, we would say.

This viewpoint opens up an interesting field for study, but unfortunately not enough surveys have been made of precognitive experiences of large-scale disasters to draw firm conclusions. We have Dr Stevenson's study of the sinking of the *Titanic* and Dr Barker's of the Aberfan disaster, and there are a certain number of cases connected with the crash of the airship R101 in France in October 1930 – two are given in Dame Edith Lyttelton's *Some Cases of Prediction* – but these are hardly sufficient for our purposes. I will return to this point in the penultimate chapter which deals with the work of the British Premonitions Bureau.

[2] Thirty-five, in fact, were listed by Dr Barker in the *Journal* of the SPR.

4 A crash in the mountains

On the morning of 17 August 1956, Mr Jack Roberts (pseudonym) looked from the windows of the Tequendama Hotel in Bogotá, Colombia, at the mountain range of the Andes, in an undecided state of mind. He was visiting Bogotá, which is on a high plateau between two ranges of the Andes, as the representative of an important British firm with a large export business, and at midnight the previous night had agreed to join some local businessmen in a flight to Tunja, one hundred miles north east of them, to inspect a factory.

However, when Mr Roberts returned to the hotel after the meeting, Mrs Gisela Hass (pseudonym), a close friend who was staying there, and whom he intended to marry, begged him not to go.

That night Mr Roberts slept well but Mrs Hass was so ill in the morning that she 'looked green', as he expressed it to me when we met in London in 1973. She told him that she had not slept all night and in the early hours of the morning, while in a drowsy state of mind, she had seen in a vision a small plane crash in the mountains. Again she entreated him not to go on the flight.

Mr Roberts was undecided. This was understandable. He had promised to go on a business trip and he could not think of any adequate reason for changing his mind.

Mrs Hass sensed his mood.

'If you go, I shan't stay here,' she declared. 'You had better pack your clothes and take them to a friend.'

The clouds hanging low over the mountains gave them a threatening look. Mrs Hass was now so ill that he felt he could not leave her.

'Very well. I'll cancel the trip,' he decided.

Mr Roberts went down to the foyer of the hotel and told Mr Roger Vaughan, a director of the firm which had invited him to inspect the factory, that he could not accompany him and Mr Hernandez, another director, on the flight, and suggested that it should be postponed.

However Mr Vaughan said he had urgent reasons for visiting the factory that day and the trip could not be postponed.

Mr Roberts was not the only one to suggest that the flight should be postponed. The pilot of the Cessna which was to take the party to Tunja, Captain Buitrago, aged 35 and highly experienced, also said it would be wise to wait, but his view was based on an appraisal of the threatening weather.

It was eventually decided that the trip should go ahead as planned. An hour and a half after the Cessna took off from the airfield, 9,000 feet above sea level, it crashed near Choconta and all in the plane were killed. The crash was seen by villagers, who reported it to the authorities.

In the meantime Mr Roberts was being taken by his friend, a devout Roman Catholic, to three churches to pray for the safety of the passengers in the plane, so certain was she that it would crash. Although he did not share her religious views, he joined her in her prayers.

When news of the crash reached the British Embassy at Bogotá, inquiries were made about Mr Roberts's safety, as it was known that he was to have been in the plane, but no certain answer was possible as the remains could not be identified. Officials from the British Embassy telephoned the Tequendama Hotel, but as Mr Roberts was not there it was assumed that he had gone on the flight, and the head office of his firm in London was notified of his death.

However, as a precaution, the Embassy officials kept telephoning the hotel throughout the day, and they finally made contact with Mr Roberts forty minutes after midnight. It was then that the pilot's reluctance to make the flight was explained to him.

Mr Roberts promptly sent a cable to his employers to assure them that he was alive.

He entered details of this strange incident in his diary which is still in his possession.

Mr Roberts told me that Mrs Hass is mainly of German

descent, but she also has Hungarian, French and Italian blood. She is tall and blonde, was a ballet dancer and instructor in gymnastics, and shared with him a love of music. She was legally separated from her husband, a diplomat from another country in South America.

Mrs Hass's gift for foretelling the future saved her life and that of her husband and mother when they were together in Hamburg, where Mr Hass had a consular post, during the war. She had a dream which caused her to warn her husband and mother that they must move immediately because 'this [the district] will not be here tomorrow.' Her mother heard this with resentment, as she was a zealous Roman Catholic and disliked her daughter's belief in her psychic gifts, but she had had enough evidence of them in the past not to protest too much when her son-in-law decided that they should move. Mrs Hass also telephoned her sister in Heidelberg telling her of her dream.

Two nights after the dream, the area of Hamburg in which the Hass family had been living was flattened by the first of the massed bomber raids which are now so much a matter of controversy.

Mrs Hass bought new furniture for the flat which her husband had taken in another part of the city, but once again she had a dream in which she saw that district of Hamburg flattened. The family moved out during the night, just before the biggest bomber raid of all devastated the district. The second dream preceded the bomber raid by twenty-four hours.

When Mr Roberts visited Germany with Mrs Hass, he had confirmation from her mother and sister that they had been told about the dreams which had caused the family to move *before* the bombing raids which had twice destroyed their flats took place.

Mr Roberts had personal experience of Mrs Hass's strange gifts once more in 1956. It was during the week which preceded the Hungarian uprising in October. They were then in South America.

'I could not control her. She was complaining all the time and could not sleep properly,' he told me. 'Three days before the uprising she said to me "I keep dreaming of people in black and people carrying coffins. It's in a city but I don't know where it is." '

However, Mrs Hass thought that her experience could relate to something that would happen in central Europe, and asked Mr Roberts to send a night cable to her mother and sister in Baden-Baden asking them to look out for 'something terrible that is going to happen.'

Mr Roberts sent the cable. The following day the Hungarian uprising started. Although Mrs Hass had been so troubled on the preceding night that she could not sleep, she became calmer when she discovered the source of her fears.

I had a number of interviews with Mr Roberts, who impressed me as being a good and honest witness. At my request he searched until he found the diary with the relevant details about the crash of the Cessna in Colombia. The case would obviously be stronger if Mrs Hass could be interviewed, but this is not possible because of distance. Mr Roberts has shown me letters (in German) from Mrs Hass as proof of her identity.

As long ago as 1937, Dame Edith Lyttelton was able to write in *Some Cases of Prediction* (Bell): 'Prevision about accidents to aeroplanes seems not uncommon, perhaps because we are not yet thoroughly accustomed to them.' We are certainly accustomed to them now, however.[1]

The next case concerns the death of Stuart Bentine, aged 21, the son of the comedian Michael Bentine, in a plane piloted by another young man, in which he was a passenger, on 28 August 1971. The plane disappeared after take-off from an airfield in Hampshire. Nine weeks later the wreckage of the plane, and the bodies of the two young men, were discovered in a wood sixteen miles away.

In an interview with Mr James Green, of the London *Evening News*, Mr Bentine said:

Before my son Stuart was killed in that plane crash I had a clear precognition of what was going to happen to him.

I told Stuart about it and his mother was present. She was upset and I ought not to have said anything while she was there.

I warned him to take care and I had never before warned him in his life. I never tried to stop him because the individual must have free choice.

The precognition came during the day – 12 weeks before the crash

[1] In 1972 there were 41 fatal air accidents throughout the world with 1,285 deaths.

– and I saw clearly the aircraft, saw it flying into cloud and then crash into the ground. All that was missing was when it would happen.

This clearly was a visionary experience. I wrote to Mr Bentine for confirmation of this account, but he was away at the time and my letter was acknowledged by Mrs Bentine. I made a number of efforts to interview him but all were unsuccessful, doubtless because he was busy. I would not have published this account but for the fact that Mrs Bentine confirmed to me over the telephone that she was present when her son was warned by his father about what was going to happen to him.

She added, 'He often gets these things and it's nerve racking to live with. But they are not all gloomy. Sometimes they are glad ones.'[2]

Britain's greatest air disaster was the crash of a British European Airways Trident at 5.11 p.m. (local time) on 18 June 1972, near Staines, Middlesex, a few minutes after it had taken off from London (Heathrow) Airport for Brussels. All on board, 118, were killed.

A week later *The Observer* carried an interview with the wife of one of those killed in the crash, Dr John Raeside.

Mrs Raeside said that her husband had a premonition of disaster. 'It was not that he thought he would be killed, he just felt very strongly that he didn't want to go to the conference,' she told Linda Blandford, a staff writer, 'but with me it was more clear. I had the premonition that something would go wrong. As I got home I turned on the radio and knew he was dead before I heard it.'

The scale of this disaster made me think that possibly it was accompanied by a number of premonitions. I appealed for reports of these in a letter in *The Observer*. A number of replies were received claiming experiences of various kinds which could possibly apply to the crash, but on analysis most of these had to be rejected.

One interesting experience for which there was confirmation was that of Mrs Monica Clarke, of Letchworth, Hertfordshire, who wrote:

On the night of Saturday 17 June I went to bed in a somewhat troubled state of mind regarding one or two close family matters, and

[2]Since this book was published in England I have met Mr Michael Bentine and he confirms my account of the circumstances surrounding the death of his son.

I dreamt very vividly, all connected with things on my mind that I could account for. But, just before I wakened, I dreamt I was with a friend – we were sitting on a seat in the country, although not far distant were tall buildings. The sky became suddenly darkened and oppressive. Without warning, there was a bright flash of lightning and an aircraft seemed to fall from nowhere out of the sky into a field very near where we were sitting. After a few seconds it seemed to burst into flames. Prior to this there had been no sound of an aircraft's engine. At this point I wakened. I was very troubled and shaken and immediately had to get up and tell my husband and daughter of what seemed a nightmare.

The dream was on my mind all day that Sunday; in fact my daughter and I sat for over an hour in the afternoon discussing how I could possibly dream of a crashing aircraft when everything else I could connect with my waking thoughts. At six o'clock we heard on the radio the news of the crash. . . . I have never had an experience like this before. I would not say that I am a particularly calm person, as I do worry a great deal over trivialities and large problems alike.

Miss Susannah Clarke, aged seventeen, wrote:

I have read the letter my mother is sending you and write myself to confirm the content. On that Sunday morning she woke me up earlier than usual, and obviously very distressed. She described the dream to me and, as we are both interested in the various theories of our 'dream' life we attempted to explain it as symbolism, but it just did not fit. All day she was very worked up and kept talking about it. Finally, when we heard the news on the radio, she was very relieved, and kept mentioning how various parts of the dream fitted in. . . .

It is worth noting that Mrs Clarke had never had an experience like this before. The dream obviously had a profound effect on her. 'It was so real,' she told me on the telephone.

In the afternoon of the day when the Trident crashed, Miss Eliot Bliss was lying down in her home in Bishop's Stortford, Hertfordshire, on the point of going to sleep for an hour (she had been very ill), when the word 'Trident' flashed through her mind, accompanied by a 'snap shot' picture of this plane, but on the ground.

'Curious, I wonder why I thought that,' she mused before dropping off to sleep. The time when she had what she described as 'this rather slight' experience was certainly ten minutes past four, as just before this she had to take medicine.

She heard the news of the crash on the six o'clock news. 'This is not much of a "premonition", but it is obviously something in the nature of one, though the "information" I got was very incomplete,' she wrote to me.

Miss Bliss did not tell anyone about her experience at the time as it seemed rather slight. She did not usually talk about her ESP experiences, particularly as she was seeing few people then because of her illness.

Miss Bliss is a member of the SPR and I called at her home to discuss her many experiences involving extra-sensory perception. She is a careful observer, widely read in the literature of the subject, and keeps notes of the more significant experiences. I have no hesitation in accepting her account of the Trident incident, slight though it is. It will be noted that she had it an hour before the plane crashed.

Miss Bliss wrote:

Most of my precognitive visions seem to have been personal and to do with my own life. I rarely have precognition of public events, though this has happened as you will see.[3] A lot of things I pick up in dreams, though some in a half-waking state. Most of my ESP experiences seem to be picked up at the time when they are happening, and often in an oblique way, though some the day before I read them in the paper! These are nearly always about people in whom I'm already interested, sometimes know, but am not in touch with by normal means. Since 1970 I started to be very ill and hardly ever out of pain and twice near death and all ESP experiences ceased for a while, so it seems as if one needs a certain degree of health to have them, or I do.

My appeal for experiences about the Trident crash brought an interesting letter from Mrs Jean Jones, of Walton-le-Dale, Preston, Lancashire. While it did not relate directly to the Trident, it contained a telling point about a feeling of unease experienced by a young boy before a flight, one possibly similar to that of Dr Raeside. Mrs Jones, who is a graduate, wrote in 1972 as follows:

Seven years ago I was living in London and my eldest son was living in Preston with his father from whom I was divorced. My son at this time was nine years old and occasionally he would visit me in Ealing, flying from Manchester in charge of a stewardess.

[3]One such experience is given at the end of chapter nine.

On one occasion when he was due to return home we were in rather a rush to catch the flight from Heathrow to Manchester. When we were almost at the airport my son told me that he felt very uneasy. I attributed this to the fact that he thought he was going to miss the plane but he told me that it wasn't that but a vague uneasiness which he could not explain. In fact, we were so late at the airport that the transport bus had left, but, when I explained that someone would be meeting my son at Manchester and would they be able to get a message to the lounge there that he would be on the next plane, a special car took my son to catch the original booked flight.

Since my son was only young it was our practice to phone each other when he arrived safely. On this particular occasion the phone call was later than usual but I merely assumed that the journey from Manchester to Preston had taken longer than normal. When I did receive the call it was for some totally other reason.

Apparently, on arriving at Manchester airport the plane had circled several times and the fire engines and ambulances had gone out on to the tarmac. It transpired that the plane had some difficulty in lowering the wheels for landing and had circled for about twenty minutes trying to correct the fault. Fortunately it was able to make a safe landing and my son quite revelled in the drama of the situation.

I immediately recalled his feeling of apprehension and unaccountable unease on the way to Heathrow and I know that in future I would take account of such apparently unexplainable feelings.

It would be interesting, to me, if such premonitions as people experience are limited to travel as they are the ones of which there seem to be more accounts.

I wonder, especially, if this is so in view of the fact that twelve months ago my same son was trapped down a pot hole and it was five hours before the mountain rescue team could free him. Fortunately, he always wears a wet suit and without this would have undoubtedly suffered from exposure – but on this occasion he had no sense of unease.

To me, it was quite inexplicable that a boy of nine years old, with no dread of flying, should have felt apprehension and I would indeed be very interested in the accounts of premonitions which you gather and for possible explanations.

This chapter started with an account of a plane crash in the Andes and will end with one of a crash on a wooded mountain at Hochwald, near Basle, Switzerland. The plane concerned was a chartered Vanguard and in it, beside the crew, were 144 passengers, mostly women from four Somerset villages. Of those on board, 107 lost their lives when the plane came down in a blinding snowstorm on 10 April 1973.

At least five Mendip villagers claimed that they had premonitions that 'something was wrong' with the day trip to Switzerland and because of these forebodings of disaster they stayed at home. I have been unable to get details of all these cases, but one obtained a good deal of publicity at the time and it is worth giving again, particularly as I have been able to get confirmation of it.

Mrs Marian Warren, a farmer's wife, aged 34, of Churchill Green, near Bristol, told reporters that she foresaw the death flight of the Vanguard in a dream three weeks in advance and as a result sold her ticket at half price.

She said, 'It was all so clear in my dream. I saw the aeroplane come over some trees and crash into the snow. There were bodies of my friends being laid out. It was vivid and horrible. I felt cold all day despite sitting in front of a big fire.'

Mrs Warren made an excuse to the organizer of the trip and returned her ticket. She did not tell anyone about the dream, apart from one friend, 'because I thought no one would believe me.'

The friend she told was Mrs Lorraine Tilley, who lives in nearby Yatton. Mrs Tilley said, 'Mrs Warren and I were talking about all sorts of things and then she told me about the aeroplane crash she had seen in a dream. I thought nothing more about it until I heard the news. Then I was shocked. The conversation I'd had with Marian came back so vividly.'

A member of the SPR in Bristol rang Mrs Warren at my request and was told that she had a precognitive dream about a plane crash which caused her to change her mind about going on the trip. Mr Kenneth Tew, a journalist on the staff of the London *Evening Standard* whom I have known for many years, told me how he had interviewed Mrs Tilley to obtain confirmation of her conversation with Mrs Warren about her dream. 'If I had not had this confirmation I would not have printed the story,' Mr Tew, who is a most conscientious journalist, told me.

The evidence in this case is good. It is not surprising that Mrs Warren was reluctant to talk about her dream. Although it had

had a considerable impact on her she could not expect other people to be convinced by it.

I will return to the subject of air disasters in the chapter on the British Premonitions Bureau.

5 A pre-view of a wartime airfield

When Wing Commander (now Air Marshal Sir Victor) Goddard spent a week-end in North Berwick in 1935, he became involved in one of the strangest experiences of his life; certainly nothing like it had happened to him before and it can have had few, if any, parallels elsewhere.

He flew up from Andover, where he was the staff officer in charge of the operational policy of No. 3 Bomber Group, and landed his Hawker Hart aeroplane at Turnhouse (now Edinburgh Airport). On the Sunday he went with his hostess, Mrs Peploe, to Drem to see if it might be practicable another time to land his aircraft on the old disused airfield there, known to him in the first world war, instead of on the far side of Edinburgh.

They called at the farm where the owner lived and with his permission inspected the place. There were four hangars laid out in line, three sets of double hangars and one single. These were of a standard type to be seen in various parts of the country as first world war airfield constructions. However, the roofs were falling in and they were in no state to house aircraft. The tarmac was in sad disrepair and the airfield itself was divided up by barbed wire fences into numerous pastures, with large numbers of cattle grazing. Obviously the place could not be used as an airport.

On the Monday morning, Sir Victor (as I will now call him) drove to Turnhouse. He described what happened then in an article headed 'Breaking the time barrier' in *Light*, the journal of The College of Psychic Studies, London, in the summer of 1966. He wrote:

I was somewhat depressed by the state of low clouds and rain, knowing that I had to fly over mountainous country in an open aircraft, without radio navigational aids or cloud-flying instruments; nevertheless I felt confident that I could get through. I believed that I should be able to fly above a low layer of clouds, in the space between that layer and an upper layer. But when I took off and climbed there was no gap; continuous clouds persisted to over 8,000 feet, where I began to be aware that I was out of control and coming down in a spiral – a state of flying I found I was unable to correct. I could make the spiralling faster or less fast, but I could not bring the aircraft into a condition where the compass ceased to spin. I was losing height rapidly and was unaware of my position, or whether I should strike mountains before I came out of the clouds. When the altimeter showed 1,000 feet I appreciated that unless I quickly came out of the clouds I was heading for disaster. The air was getting very dark indeed, and the clouds had become yellowish brown and drenching with rain. At two hundred feet only, spiralling steeply, I began to see a murky sort of daylight and immediately emerged over 'rotating' water which instantaneously I knew to be the Firth of Forth.

In a moment I saw, rotating slowly from right to left, a stone sea-wall carrying a road, path and railings. Falling so rapidly, I was almost instantaneously level with it, turning head-on into it – it had a high stone wall at back, beyond which I could not see. I would have struck the railing, the road or the back wall had I not instantly regained my orientation and sense of the vertical, thanks to the railings on the esplanade, and a girl who was running in pouring rain with a pram – she had to duck her head to miss my wing-tip! This shaking experience enabled me to check my spiralling in the nick of time before I struck the sea-wall, and then to clear the railing and finally to lift the nose before striking the water, which I only just avoided. I whistled rapidly over the stony beach in pouring rain which obscured any distant view of the country beyond.

Flying at 150 miles an hour in an open cockpit aeroplane with heavy rain driving on one's forehead and flying goggles is not only painful but very difficult, especially as I could not go other than close to the ground (20-30 feet) because of the very low cloud (about 40-60 feet). I was determined to head straight on to identify my position for, with my compass swinging, I did not know which side of the Firth of Forth I might be. The easiest landmark to find would be, I presumed, Drem airfield where I had been only the day before. In a few minutes I was aware of my position. I identified the road to Edinburgh, and soon after saw looming through the gloom the black silhouettes of the Drem hangars. In a moment I was over the airfield boundary in deluging rain and in very dark, turbulent flying conditions.

On crossing the boundary, the airfield and all my immediate surroundings were miraculously bathed in full sunlight, as it seemed to me; the rain had ceased, the hangars were nearby, their north-west end doors open. Lined out in spick and span order on a newly laid tarmac were four aeroplanes: three bi-planes of a standard flying-training type of aircraft called Avro 504N; one monoplane of an unknown type. We had at that time no monoplanes in the RAF, but the one I saw then was of the type which thereafter I carried in my memory and identified with the Magister which became, later on, a 'trainer'. Another peculiarity about the aeroplanes on the tarmac was that they were painted bright chrome yellow. All aircraft in the RAF in 1935 were exclusively aluminium-doped; there were no yellow aeroplanes. Later, because of an alarming increase in fatal accidents at flying training schools during the first phase of the expansion of the Air Force, the need became apparent for making training aircraft easily seen: in 1938 and 1939, more probably the latter, yellow aeroplanes became universal at all RAF flying training schools.

In the mouth of the hangar closest to me another monoplane was being wheeled out. The mechanics pushing it were wearing blue overalls. As I passed over them, having climbed from only a few feet above ground to just high enough to clear the roof of the hangar, I must have been making a great deal of noise and, normally, this would have caused a considerable sensation. Zooming the hangars, as I was doing, was a court-martial offence! It was quite certain that those mechanics must have looked up at me (had I been 'there' to them) as I flew over so close. But none of them looked up. This struck me as very strange. It also struck me as strange that the airmen were wearing blue overalls. RAF mechanics had never worn anything but brown overalls when working in hangars on aircraft. The hangar roofs, above which I was flying a moment later, were gleaming with the wetness of recent rain, but the bituminous fabric was entirely new and in very good order. Also the tarmac all around the hangars was new.

I don't now recall any other particularly novel or interesting technical features, but I remember that, at the time, there were many points quickly seen which struck me as unusual, anomalous – and non-existent at Drem the day before. The line of hangars was not more than a hundred and sixty yards long from end to end. To fly that length would only take a few seconds. I was then immediately confronted once more with deluging rain, turbulent semi-darkness and the prospect of having, once more, to climb through continuous cloud over mountains.

The airfield I had just seen was in splendid order for aircraft. I saw no aircraft actually using it; but there were no longer any barbed-wire fences, no grazing sheep or cattle; the surface was evenly green and recently mown. It was clearly a first-rate grass airfield. I do not recall it having a runway. As I was confronted with storm and the need to get on with my journey, it may be asked why, if the airfield was in such a good state and the weather conditions so bad, did I not seek to land? The reason could be that I didn't believe my eyes. It could be that the thought of landing never occurred to me. Why land when conditions for flying had suddenly become so splendid? The turbulent return of dark storm may have convinced me of having had an hallucination, but I do not remember having that thought. I may have been so imbued with the sense of duty and the urgency of not abusing the privilege of week-end flying, that I decided to press on regardless. Moreover, I had some personal conceit about bad-weather flying and, despite my recent failure to master a climb through a deep cloud mass, I reckoned I could get through, and so I went on.

In fact, I climbed that time, satisfactorily, to about 17,000 feet and, somewhat gasping and very cold, flew over the clouds in bright sunlight. Actually, to test myself, I flew for a while at 21,000 feet, so I must have been physically very fit.

I landed at Andover about 11 o'clock. At the Officers' Mess I found a group of officers who had come in for 'break'. I sat with them for a while, talking about the week-end. Rashly – but I was feeling elated – I reported my extraordinary experience at Drem. We were all Wing Commanders. One of them was Wing Commander C. A. Stevens, another was Wing Commander Haylock. Wing Commander Stevens died as an Air Marshal (he should not be confused with Air Vice-Marshal A. C. Stephens). There may have been one other present.

They were amused by my story, thought it a 'tall' one, and Stevens advised me to take less whisky next time I went to Scotland for a week-end. Having heard my own story with, as it were, *their* ears, I myself became aware of its unbelievableness, and therefore did not repeat it to anyone else. An officer hardly wants to get a reputation for having hallucinations in the air; it was easy to be taken off flying for medical reasons, and I would not have liked my state of mental order to be called in question. I did, however, write and tell my hostess that I had arrived safely after having an extraordinary experience, which I briefly narrated. She also, when I asked her later (although she had forgotten the gist) remembered having thought it all very peculiar, and that I was peculiar in having it. Confirmation from her at this time is, I fear, not available, short of hypnosis. Wing Commander Haylock has recently confirmed hearing my story of the vision the same day.

Sir Victor, who has long been a member of the College of

Psychic Studies, discussed in *Light* aspects of his strange experience under the heading of 'Factual considerations and hypotheses'.

None of his hearers at Andover was appointed to the Air Ministry and therefore none was involved in any decisions affecting the development of Drem, he said. He went on:

The menace of the rise of Hitler soon gave rise to expansion plans for the RAF, and no doubt these involved the rehabilitation of disused abandoned airfields. Quite a number of old airfield installations were retained on the World War I lay-out; the hangars were refettled and put into use again. But in other cases the hangars were pulled down, and this happened at Drem. The place was rebuilt, and reopened as a flying training school in 1939, equipped with *yellow* 504N bi-planes and Magister monoplanes exactly similar to the types I had seen. By that time, also, airmen were dressed in blue overalls when at work. The airfield was cleared and the farmer was displaced, and so on. I didn't actually go to see for myself; I was told that Drem had been turned into an Elementary Flying Training School, and so I knew that it must have all the standard equipment for such a school; they were standardized throughout the Air Force. But the man who told me about the rebuilding of the place told me also that the hangars had been rebuilt. He probably did not mean (as I supposed) 'repaired'. He may well have meant 'replaced by new hangars,' but the word rebuilt serves either meaning. I, ready to believe that my vision had been fulfilled in that respect also, simply accepted what he said.

When Sir Victor was in Scotland in November 1964 he went to Drem and found that the hangars that were there then were of steel construction, covered with corrugated iron. They had been built in another pattern but were on the site of the old hangars, which had disappeared altogether.

Sir Victor said:

RAF expansion plans were prepared year by year. One very large plan, of which I wasn't aware until I enquired into this matter quite recently, embraced a lot of airfields. Drem could have been in that plan, to be rebuilt as it stood. If so, one of the people who considered that plan could, at some time, have visualized Drem airfield being rebuilt in that World War I pattern. Optimism and other factors prevailed on the Government of the day not to go so far with their expansion of the Air Force as that plan required, and much of it was put into abeyance. Later on, I have also recently learned, that plan was hurriedly revamped and the full expansion was begun once more. But by that time the supply of bricks and bricklayers may have been getting short, and the supply of corrugated iron and rolled steel joists for making steel hangars seemed to be more satisfactory and perhaps cheaper. If so, that may have been why the hangars were built on a different plan and why the old hangars were pulled down after all. Or it may have been, of course, that the new hangars being wider and of better design for modern purposes, were preferred, and no financial objection was seen to their being substituted.

However all that may be, I do not know whether Drem Airfield (Fenton Barns of World War I) was actually in any of the major plans of expansion. I feel sure that it must have been and, therefore, that it could have been in a plan for repair at one time and a plan for replacement at another. Leaving aside the unfulfilment of the hangar aspect of the vision, we are left with a good deal of what I saw of novelty being fulfilled some four or five years later. In regard to the fulfilled items, the vision could be said to be precognitive of material facts of construction and actuality. But because of the 'unfulfilled' hangars, the vision might be entirely one of precognition of ideas. I may have seen intentions as they were later to be imagined by others, but certainly not as already imagined by anyone on earth when I had the vision.

In regard to the aeroplanes, those facts-to-be were not only displaced in time, they were displaced in space; for aeroplanes would not actually be wheeled out of, and parked close outside, hangars which weren't there. In actuality, the yellow aeroplanes would be lined up outside the new steel hangars – that is, elsewhere than where I saw them. So those visionary aeroplanes, factual in regard to their future state of being, were not factual in regard to their future parking position. But they and the airmen handling them were exceedingly real.

Sir Victor pointed out that in 1935 the RAF was still taking surplus army overalls, which were brown; there was no prospect, that he was aware of, of any change because for many items of equipment the RAF depended on army supplies. The decision to change airmen's overalls from brown to blue could have been made by a member of the Equipment Staff of the Air Ministry without reference to the Air Staff. The Air Council (not the Air Staff) would perhaps be informed by the Member for Supply. But a decision to change the colour of aeroplanes from aluminium-dope to chrome-yellow would certainly involve the Air Staff almost exclusively, until, later on, a quite different branch of the Equipment Staff from that concerned with clothing would be instructed to provision for repainting training aeroplanes yellow, and the technical staff would be instructed to get the work done. The shape and style of hangars would be a concern of the Air Staff, but an accurate visualization of hangars would be much more the concern of the Works and Building Staff.

'So I would suggest that what I observed was not a reflection of one man's thinking, but the plans and intentions of many', said Sir Victor.

He continued:

As to the quality of the experience and its relation to normal reality or to dreamland, there was something ethereal about the sunlight; it was brilliant and glorious, but yet somewhat other than normal bright sunlight. I had a strange feeling about the mechanics on the ground as real men. Although quite real in their movements and general manner towards their job, looking quite natural, yet they did not react naturally towards me and my zooming Hart close overhead. Evidently they neither saw nor heard me. But I could see both my aeroplanes *and* them, at the same time. Afterwards I wondered whether, in the context, they were more real than I was! But I had remained flying in my aeroplane; I was not disembodied. I was aware of my change of circumstances but also of the noise that my aeroplane made, and I was aware of the appropriate sensations as I swooped out over the hangars. I was not in any degree unconscious of my actions. I had, however, been suffering from mental shock and was certainly under stress of anxiety. I had been really frightened by the loss of control in the cloud, by the near certainty of death, and by the experience at the sea-wall, and I continued to be highly tensed by the rigours of the flying conditions.

It is hard to be definite in what one says about sensing the difference between a dream and a vision. The yellow aeroplanes seemed to be totally real. So did the gleaming hangar roofs, black like the backs of great whales only a few feet beneath me. They were real in the sense that one doesn't feel things to be real in a dream, as a rule. But I cannot define the distinction. There was nothing fantastical about anything I saw.

Before I discuss the implications of Sir Victor's experience over Drem airfield in which precognition seemed to be involved, I will relate another strange story. This time Sir Victor was the subject of someone else's precognitive experience. The story was first told in the *Saturday Evening Post* (Philadelphia) on 26 May 1951, and has been repeated in condensed form in a number of other publications. It was also the subject of a popular film, *The Night My Number Came Up*, but, as Sir Victor pointed out to me, various script writers had made significant changes to the story.

The other person involved was a senior naval officer, who appeared in Sir Victor's original narrative under the pseudonym of Commander Dewing. His ship was given as HMS *Crecy*. His name has never been revealed since then, but he was in fact Captain Gerald Gladstone, in command of the cruiser HMS *Black Prince* at Shanghai. Captain Gladstone had a most distinguished career in the Royal Navy and, when he retired in 1960 as the oldest serving officer, he was Admiral Sir Gerald Gladstone. From 1955 to 1957, he was Commander of the Allied Naval Forces in Northern Europe and from 1957 to 1960 Commander-in-Chief of the Far East Station.

Sir Victor was kind enough to put me in touch with the Admiral, who invited me to his home in Dorset to discuss the case and to examine the correspondence he had with Sir Victor about it. They are substantially in agreement about the precognitive experience which caused Captain Gladstone, as he was then, to think that the Air Marshal was dead, but after that there are significant differences in the accounts.

Before I discuss the possible reason for these differences, I will give in slightly condensed form Sir Victor's account of what took place in Shanghai at a cocktail party given in his honour in January, 1946. Sir Victor, who had commanded the Royal New Zealand Air Force during the war before going on to administer British Air Forces for the reconquest of Burma and Malaya, was in Shanghai in the course of a farewell tour. He says:

The room was loosely thronged and there was an easy Anglo-American clatter of conversation. I was talking with Sally Dean and her future husband, my old friend Brig. Gen. John McConnell, USAF, when I heard two Englishmen behind me begin a conversation which caught my attention at once. It ran like this:

'I'm very glad this party is really on tonight!'
'Of course, old boy, but why shouldn't it be?'
'Well, wasn't it laid on to welcome Air Marshal Goddard?'
'It certainly was. What of it?'
'We haven't met him. We never shall. He's dead!'
'Dead. You don't mean that! He couldn't be. Ogden (Mr George

Alyne Ogden, the British Consul General) would have put off the party.'

'Yes, that's what I thought. But he is dead. Died last night in a crash – hell of a crash. Yes, he was killed – no doubt about that. . . .'

The man spoke with a disconcerting tone of authority. *Is he crazy,* I wondered, *or am I hearing things*? I turned my body slowly half left. Before I had time to take in the man's appearance, he glanced quickly at my face and started as though I had hit him.

'My God!' he exclaimed with a gasp. 'I'm terribly sorry! I mean I'm terribly glad – that is – how extraordinary and how appalling! I do apologize!'

He was a British naval officer, a commander. I smiled and said, 'I may be a bit moribund, Commander, but I'm not quite dead yet. What made you think I was?'

He hesitated. And then he spoke quite definitely. 'I dreamt it. I had a dream! Last night . . . or was it this afternoon? I could have sworn it was true. It seemed so true. How frightful!'

'What else did you dream about?' I asked – I had more than the obvious reason for being interested. 'Where did it happen?'

'It was on a rocky, shingly shore, in the evening, in storm. It was awful, snowstorm. Don't know whether it was China or Japan. You'd been over the mountains in cloud. Up a long time . . . I watched it all happen.'

According to Sir Victor, the naval officer said that in addition to the Royal Air Force crew the plane that crashed – 'an ordinary sort of transport passenger plane. Might have been a Dakota' – was carrying three civilians, two men and a woman. All were English.

Both officers had read Dunne's *An Experiment with Time* and discussed his theory about a time limit for dreams that seemed to come true. Dunne's own words are: 'Obviously, even a dream of a pile of sixpences upsetting off a red book would be likely to be matched by a similar waking experience, if one allowed oneself the whole of one's life in which to look for the matching. A bank clerk might even find fulfilment in a fortnight. I decided that two days should be the accepted limit; *but that this might be extended in ratio to the oddity and unusualness of the incident*'.

So much for the cocktail party.

That evening the Consul General gave a dinner party for Sir Victor, who had thought it impossible that the plane assigned to take him to Tokyo would be called on to carry three civilians, but he had already promised to take the Hon. Seymour Berry, of the *Daily Telegraph*, with him, and in the course of the dinner he met requests for a passage from Mr Ogden himself, who was wanted urgently in Tokyo, and finally by Ogden again, but this time on behalf of the British representative in Tokyo, to take a stenographer there. With some reluctance Sir Victor agreed that the stenographer should come. She was Miss Dorita Breakspear, aged about twenty.

The Dakota, with eleven people on board, left Shanghai airport early the following morning for Japan. After a dreadful flight in cloud, some of it over the mountains of Japan, the captain of the Dakota crash-landed the plane in the early evening on the rocky, shingly shore of an island off the coast of Japan, in a snowstorm. All survived.

Now for Sir Gerald's account. He told me that he woke up on the morning of the party convinced that the Air Marshal was dead. He was unable to account for this conviction because he had never had an experience like this before nor has he since. If the conviction was conveyed by anything he had seen in a dream no memory of it remained. All that day he expected to be told of the Air Marshal's death, but when no news was received he went to the cocktail party which was being given in Sir Victor's honour in the VIP guest-house by a Wing Commander, the local representative of the RAF, whose name he does not remember.

Sir Gerald said he was among the first guests to arrive and told the Wing Commander that he was glad the party was still on because he thought the Air Marshal was dead. Sir Victor, coming in after him, must have overheard this remark. 'I am sorry I did not keep my mouth shut,' Sir Gerald said ruefully in relating this incident to me.

On 2 January 1947, Sir Victor wrote to Sir Gerald about the incident, asking for details about his seemingly precognitive experience, and remarked, 'For the next forty-eight hours I was quite convinced that I was going to die and wondered how many unfortunate passengers would share the experience with me.'

Sir Gerald's reply is dated 30 January 1947. The relevant portion of his letter is as follows:

I am sorry to say that I am unable to fill in any details of the dream I had. I clearly remember now what I remembered of my dream at the time: and that was simply a conviction that YOU WERE DEAD. Being no devotee of Dunne's theories, and too lazy anyway, I have never made a point as he did of recalling every detail of my dreams the instant I awake. If I had acquired the ability possibly I would be in a position to give some reason for the conviction which was all that remained with me, in fact, when I awoke. But knowing the silly way dreams usually behave I can well believe that they would be totally different from anything which, in fact, happened to you. . . .

I heard, of course, at the time of your crash and had the details from Ogden, to whom (and to his wife) I offered my deepest apologies for the alarm I must have caused them. I do hope you also will accept them. . . .

The two officers were in touch again in 1950 when Sir Victor, who had been approached by the *Saturday Evening Post*, sent a copy of his narrative to Sir Gerald for his comments. The Admiral has kept a copy of his reply in which he suggested various amendments. His suggested version of how the conversation at the cocktail party should read includes the following:

'I'm very glad the party is on tonight.'

'Of course, old boy, but why shouldn't it be?'

'Well, it was laid on to welcome Goddard, as you know, and I woke up this morning utterly convinced Goddard was dead. Only a dream I suppose, but so astonishingly forceful that I really honestly expected to be called up and told it was all off. I mean I wouldn't have been the least bit surprised to hear he'd crashed or something. And, so, I'm very glad he hasn't and the party is on.'

I (Goddard) turned to look at the speaker. He was a naval captain. I smiled and said, 'What's all this about me being dead. I may be a bit moribund but I'm not quite dead yet. What made you think I was?'

He hesitated and then said, 'I say, I'm dreadfully sorry. What a silly thing to say. I suppose I dreamed it. I don't remember how or what. But I woke up this morning quite certain you were dead.'

'What else did you dream about?' I asked (I had more than obvious reasons for being interested). 'Where did it happen?'

'I don't know,' he said doggedly. 'I'm afraid I don't remember any details. I just knew you were dead. I'm awfully glad you aren't,' he added with a rather sheepish smile, 'and it gives you just 48 hours.'

'Why 48 hours?' I asked.

'Well,' said the captain, 'perhaps you've read Dunne's *Experiment With Time*. You may remember he discovered that some dreams, or some bits of dreams, come true. He argued that almost everything could come true if you wait long enough, so he set a limit of 48 hours and said if it didn't come true in that time the dream was unlikely to have any relation to what happened. That's why I said you've got 48 hours – 48 hours of danger, you know.'

I remembered something of this as he spoke. As far as I recalled Dunne makes out that when the subconscious mind is released from the duty of serving the conscious mind, the conscious mind has gone off duty – gone to sleep – then the subconscious wanders off into space and time making sequence pictures to taunt the sleeping conscious mind's eye, mixing up past and future, fact and fancy. That's dreaming.

It will be seen from this extract of dialogue that the Admiral stresses once again that he does not remember any detail of his dream but that he woke up convinced that the Air Marshal was dead.

Twenty-four hours later Air Marshal Goddard was involved in a plane crash or, rather, a forced landing on the rocky shore of an island during a storm in circumstances which could easily have resulted in his death and that of all on board.

It will be seen that these two officers, both of unimpeachable integrity, agree, in essence, on what was said at the cocktail party about Captain Gladstone's strong conviction that Air Marshal Goddard – to give them both their rank at the time – was dead, but they disagreed about what was said, or was not said, after that.

Why should this be so?

For a start we must remember the circumstances in which the talk took place. It was at a cocktail party and anyone who has ever attended such functions must know how difficult it is, after the party has been going for a while, to hold a coherent conversation above the noise, the interruptions ('here's somebody you must meet' and so on), and the general reluctance, on the part of all present, to become too deeply involved in a serious topic because it interferes with what might be described as 'having a good time.' Captain Gladstone was an early arrival at the party, followed by the Air Marshal, and they talked about the strange presentiment of the crash then, but later exchanges might well have taken place when more guests were present and because of the noise there could have been a genuine misunderstanding about what was said.

We must next bear in mind the effect that the passage of time has on memory. I have little doubt that if the two officers had been able to meet over breakfast the following morning, they would have agreed on the substance of what was said. However, this was not possible. Air Marshal Goddard left on an early flight to Tokyo and Captain Gladstone sailed a few days later in his cruiser. Much had happened to both of them, immersed in their respective duties, before they corresponded a year later.

Remembering is not the simple process which many people imagine it is. For a study of the processes involved we may turn to *Remembering*, by Sir Frederick Bartlett, Professor Emeritus of Experimental Psychology at Cambridge University, published for the first time by the Cambridge University Press in 1932 and reprinted in 1950 and 1954. The book is sub-titled 'A Study in Experimental and Social Psychology.' Sir Frederick points out that remembering, like recognizing, involves (1) an original sensorial pattern; (2) an original psychological orientation, or attitude; (3) the persistence of this orientation or attitude in some setting which is different from the original at least in a temporal sense; and (4) the organization, together with orientation or attitude, of psychological material. He says that remembering, as distinct from recognizing, depends upon the possibility of exploiting the fourth of these factors much more fully. He notes on page 205 that 'as has been shown again and again, condensation, elaboration and invention are common features of ordinary remembering'. To this he adds: 'if we consider evidence rather than presupposition, remembering appears to be far more decisively an affair of construction rather than one of mere reproduction.'

This viewpoint, the result of a great deal of experimental research, is confirmed in views attributed to Mr Tom Harrisson, anthropologist and explorer and a senior research fellow at Sussex University, in an interview in *The Times* of 6 July 1973 entitled 'Eyewitness accounts of the blitz and "our finest hours"'. Mr Harrisson who founded Mass-Observation with Charles Madge in 1937, has in his archives the war diaries of 500 people and thousands of reports from a 'national panel' – a network of voluntary observers all over the country who wrote down whatever they thought worth recording and covered particular topics and events when requested to do so. Mr Harrisson tested with some of the diarists who had written to him in recent weeks their recollection of what happened to them in blitz situations. He said, 'The discrepancies with what they wrote at the time, in the material we hold in the archive, is often enormous. It might be two different people or two different events.'

Mr Harrisson's correspondents were attempting to recall events which had happened thirty years before whereas only a year had elapsed before Sir Victor and Sir Gerald tried to recall what had been said at the cocktail party in Shanghai, but it will be seen that the same difficulties apply to remembering what happened at the time. When the problem is viewed in this way it will be realized that good faith is not involved. Sir Gerald pointed out to me at his home that his recollection of an incident in his days as a midshipman differed greatly from his account of the same incident in the diary he kept at the time.

In view of the factors I have discussed here, what conclusions should we draw from this case?

My feeling is that we should concentrate on the Admiral's conviction when he woke up that morning in Shanghai, that the Air Marshal, whom he was to meet for the first time that day, was dead. So strong was the conviction that he voiced it at a cocktail party and was overheard by the 'dead' man. This incident alone makes the publication of the case by Sir Victor fully justified. It may be argued, of course, that Sir Gerald's conviction was just the result of a dream which he could not remember and that Sir Victor's plane just happened to crash and, as he was not killed, there was not really any connection between the conviction of death on the Admiral's part and the plane crash nearly forty-eight hours later. This viewpoint would carry greater weight if Sir Gerald were in the habit of waking frequently from sleep with such convictions in his mind, but he assures me that he does not. This is the one and only experience he has had of this kind and he is unable to explain it. It left him with such a strong conviction that the Air Marshal was dead that he expected all that day to be told that he had crashed and it was still very much on his mind, as we have seen, at the cocktail party in the evening. The crash was not a fatal one, fortunately, but this fact does not invalidate Sir Gerald's experience because, as I have discussed in the introduction, precognitive experiences often concern events with a probable outcome rather than a fixed one.

I am most grateful to Sir Victor and Sir Gerald for the long interviews they gave me to discuss this case and to Sir Gerald for making the correspondence relating to it available. Both have seen this account in advance.

Now we return to Sir Victor's strange experience over Drem Airfield in 1935.

In his article in *Light*, Sir Victor wrote:

The sceptic may say, 'If an intelligent man has a vision of this extraordinary kind, why doesn't he write it down and refer it to somebody who can make a proper record of it? Then when the event comes to pass, there's the cast-iron evidence. Failing that, the evidence is valueless: "All men are liars" '.

I do not suggest that serious investigators are especially prone to prejudice. Certainly they should not be gullible; on the other hand, they certainly should not be unreasonable! What normal person, never having considered visions, would think that an 'hallucination' was going to come true? Sceptics who think as I have postulated do not realise the psychology of the normal Service Officer. People in the Service just don't have hallucinations; it is not 'done'! If a man sees, in broad daylight, what is 'not there' he doesn't talk about it. He doesn't want a stigma attached to him. For his own self-respect he knows that he was sober at the time, but it would not occur to him that what he saw was likely to have any significance at all for anyone else. After telling close friends, perhaps, he would recognize that the sooner the incident was forgotten the better. So I don't think it is really fair to expect somebody who has an ESP experience for the first time, especially if he is in a profession such as mine, to take serious notice of it and write it down. Getting my leg pulled about it was quite sufficient to shut me up altogether and to suppress the memory of it until, by surprise, later on, I heard that the vision had been materialized. Then, of course, I wrote again to my North Berwick hostess and remarked on the fact that Drem had been reopened, and asked if she remembered my writing to her about it after I had stayed there in 1935? Vaguely, as related above, she said she thought she could recall something about a strange happening, but what it was she had forgotten.

Sir Victor starts his article in *Light* with the remark that, 'It is clearly important, with "ESP experiences", to give some account of the circumstances and the state of mind of the experient'. In analysing his experience over the airfield he said, 'I had been suffering from mental shock and was certainly under stress of anxiety. I had been really frightened by the loss of control in the cloud, by the near certainty of death, and by the experience at the sea-wall, and I continued to be highly tensed by the rigours of the flying conditions'.

Sir Victor had literally been within a split-second of death when he recovered control of his plane. I thought that a medical opinion on the effects of spiralling down from a height of 8,000 feet would help and referred Sir Victor's narrative to a consultant with flying experience. He replied:

Any specialist knowledge I may have would not provide an explanation for this. I cannot help resorting to the sort of explanation most people, who are interested in psychical research, adopt, when faced with experiences of this sort. His body came within thirty seconds of death.[1] His soul, to quote the song, 'went marching on' and for a short period crossed the border into the next world and so was allowed free range along the dimension of time until the progress of the aircraft into bad weather necessitated its return.

Sir Victor crossed the airfield boundary 'in deluging rain and in very dark turbulent flying conditions' to find that the airfield and all his immediate surroundings 'were miraculously bathed in full sunlight', but when he left the airfield he was 'then immediately confronted once more with deluging rain, turbulent semi-darkness and the prospect of having, once more, to climb through continuous cloud over mountains.'

I do not feel we can maintain that freak local conditions explain why the airfield was seen to be bathed in sunlight. However, if the sceptic maintains that this was so, he has to explain why an airfield which the day before had been in use as a farm with barbed-wire fences and grazing sheep and cattle, was then, in Sir Victor's words, 'in splendid order for aircraft' and 'clearly a first-rate grass airfield.' If the sceptic is particularly persistent and attempts to argue that Sir Victor was confused about his direction after his near escape from death and flew over some other airfield in the neighbourhood, he has to explain away the items which belonged to the future such as the aeroplanes painted yellow, the Magister which was not then in use, and the mechanics wearing blue instead of brown overalls.

Sir Victor gives the clue to what happened when he said that

[1] Sir Victor's comment on this was, 'At most two seconds in this case!'

'there was something ethereal about the sunlight; it was brilliant and glorious, but yet somewhat other than normal bright sunlight.' The golden quality of sunlight has been frequently noted in mystical experiences. In *Frontiers of the Unknown* I quote from Professor J. H. Whiteman who describes one of his dreams in which 'there was a general view of sunlight, golden in quality'. Golden light is not confined only to sunlight in mystical experiences. The late Mr W. E. Manning, a member of the SPR, sent me an account describing how 'on one occasion a few years before the last war I had been practising astral projection and woke up completely cataleptic. A golden light seemed to suffuse the room within a few feet of the ceiling. . . .'

Another indication that Sir Victor had a mystical experience over the airfield is given in his remark that when he landed at Andover he was feeling elated. Elation is often associated with mystical experiences. An example of this is given in *Frontiers of the Unknown* in the chapter headed 'Two strange experiences'.

All the details Sir Victor noticed when he was over the airfield were not truly precognitive. When he visited the airfield on the day before his flight he found that the roofs of the hangars 'were falling in and they were in no state for aircraft'. However, during the flight he noticed that 'the hangar roofs . . . were gleaming with the wetness of recent rain, but the bituminous fabric was entirely new and in very good order. Also the tarmac all around the hangars was new'. It was not until 1964 that Sir Victor was able to visit Drem and found, rather to his horror, 'that (the hangars) that were then there were of steel construction, covered with corrugated iron. They had been built in another pattern, but on the site of the old hangars, which had disappeared altogether'.

Sir Victor's interpretation of this is as follows:

> leaving aside the unfulfilment of the hangar aspect of the vision, we are left with a good deal of what I saw of novelty being fulfilled some four or five years later. In regard to the fulfilled items, the vision could be said to be precognitive of material facts of construction and actuality. But because of the 'unfulfilled' hangars, the vision might be entirely one of precognition of ideas. I may have seen indications as they were later to be imagined by others, but certainly not as already imagined by anyone on earth when I had the vision.

This view is probably correct. At some time between Sir

Victor's visit to Drem and the reconstruction of the airfield, officials of the Air Ministry must have considered whether the hangars could have been repaired rather than demolished and rebuilt, and it was this that Sir Victor 'latched on to' when he was over the airfield after his narrow escape from death in 1935.

There is supporting evidence for Sir Victor's account of what happened to him at Drem airfield. Sir Victor said to me in the course of correspondence that he had mentioned it to other officers at the time and one of them, Wing Commander Haylock, had recently confirmed hearing his story of the vision the same day. His experience was probably due to heightened sensitivity as the result of a near escape from death. Such points of detail as the colour of aircraft and the mechanics' overalls, if correct, are always of evidential value when a case such as this is assessed. Sir Victor, because of his high rank in the RAF, was in a privileged position to be able to make the necessary inquiries to confirm what he had seen in his vision. This is a most interesting case.

6 A dog's premonition

It was a perfect summer day on 30 June 1944, when Mrs Baines, who lived with her husband and schoolgirl daughter Audrey, then aged nearly seventeen, at 10 Melbury Gardens, Wimbledon, saw her husband off to his office. The family cocker spaniel, Merry, was in high spirits as he danced down the path with his master but the stubby tail dropped abruptly when the gate was shut in his face.

These were difficult days for the family. Flying bombs were landing on London and only twelve hours earlier one had fallen a block away, maiming many people and reducing their homes to rubble. Windows had been blown out in the Baines's home and several ceilings cracked with the result that plaster had fallen like snow on the furniture and carpets.

Mrs Baines and Audrey, who was studying at home for her school certificate, had been cleaning up for some time when they realized that the dog was nowhere to be seen. They knew that the gates were latched and a good fence prevented him from wandering off and yet the garden seemed empty. They searched the house, looking under beds and chairs and even in the larder, but to no avail. Eventually Audrey resumed the search of the garden and noticed that the plank which guarded the entrance to the bomb shelter used by the family in the early days of the war had been knocked flat. The beams of a torch brought hurriedly from the house revealed Merry curled up and obviously asleep on the lowest bunk which he had shared with the girl four years previously but never since then, as the family had abandoned the use of the shelter in the garden in favour of one under a table in the dining-room.

The garden shelter had been used for four months in the early days of the war until Mrs Baines and Audrey went with the dog to the quietness of a tiny Cornish seaside village. When the family were reunited in London early in the spring of 1941, the garden shelter had become so damp that it could not be used. Young visitors to the house seemed fascinated by the steep steps of the disused shelter, and eventually a plank was wedged across the entrance to keep them, and the family tortoises, out.

For four years the only visitor to the shelter was Mr Baines, who vainly tried to keep the water out in winter, but here was Merry asleep as though the years which had passed since he had last been there had counted for nothing.

Audrey stepped carefully on the floor of the shelter, now covered with a skin of green slime, took the dog in her arms, and sighed with relief as she emerged into the glorious sunshine. She replaced the plank, but three times that morning it was knocked down again and each time the dog was found asleep on the bunk. In her account of this incident, Miss Baines said:

> By noon my mother and I were at our wits' end to understand the fascination of this place which had been ignored for so long. Eventually we went down into the dank darkness and sat on the bunks beside Merry. Once our eyes had become accustomed to the blackness and our noses to the stench there was a strange feeling of security not found in the steel table (in the dining-room of the house).
>
> My mother suggested that maybe we were silly not to use this bunker after all for pneumonia was curable unlike the injuries from a bomb. She began to dust off the bunks and I went in search of a new bulb and to sweep the leaves from the steps. As soon as we began to take an interest in the place Merry left and spent the rest of the day about his own pursuits.

That evening the Baines family and the dog were joined in the garden shelter, so long unused, by a neighbour, Mrs Gearing, from 14 Melbury Gardens, who until then had been sharing the steel shelter under the dining-room table. At ten minutes to three, while they were asleep, a flying bomb fell outside the houses numbered 10 to 14, forming a crater on the footpath, and part of the roadway gas mains caught fire.

According to information supplied to me by the Town Clerk of the London Borough of Merton, which now administers Wimbledon, 'the damage sustained in Melbury Gardens was: nos 3-19 destroyed; nos 1, 21, 23 and 25 badly damaged; nos

10-14 demolished; nos 30-40 damage to glass and roofs; no 42 onwards, minor glass.'

As the houses occupied by the Baines family and Mrs Gearing were demolished, it is likely that they would have lost their lives if they had not been, for the first time in four years, in the bomb shelter in the garden. Numbers 12 and 14 Melbury Gardens were adjoining semi-detached houses. The Wells family who occupied number 12 were injured. They owed their lives to the fact that they were in a shelter in the back of the house.

The story of the behaviour of the spaniel Merry which caused the Baines family and Mrs Gearing to move into the garden shelter on the night their homes were demolished by a flying bomb, came to light during correspondence I had with Mr Noël Hume, an Englishman who is director of the department of archaeology in Williamsburg, Virginia. His wife is the former Miss Audrey Baines. I met Mr and Mrs Hume when they visited London. Mrs Hume related the incident about the dog and signed as correct my account of the conversation. She also sent from Virginia on her return there an unfinished draft of the incident which she had written eight years earlier.

The question of confirmation of the incident is, of course, important. Mrs Hume's parents are dead and I have been unable to trace Mrs Gearing, who is said to have moved to Bognor Regis. However, Mrs Hume put me in touch with Mrs Stella Sutcliffe, of Parkfield Avenue, Wimbledon, who at the time of the bomb incident lived in Melbury Gardens. She told me on the telephone that she remembered the incident very clearly. The family had described to her at the time how they had moved to the garden shelter the previous night because of the dog's behaviour. She knew the Baines family had been sleeping under a table shelter in the house and thought they might have been killed when their house was demolished.

Further confirmation came from Mr Robert Allwood, who was an air raid warden at Wimbledon during the war. Mr Allwood, who now lives at East Chinnock, Yeovil, Somerset, said in response to an inquiry from me:

Your letter brought back memories of nights spent watching for flying bombs.

Mr Baines with his wife and Audrey had a shelter in the garden and also a table shelter in the house. They had used the indoor shelter for some time until the Hun got a bit too close with six bombs. Merry, the dog, said this is a bit thick and went to the garden dugout and refused to go in the house so they all took shelter in the garden. A flying bomb fell in the road and their house and two others became a heap of rubble.

Animals seem to have a sixth sense when any danger is near. The family escaped injury thanks to the dog.

The family certainly escaped injury, and possibly death, because of the dog, but is there some other explanation, apart from precognition of danger, for the dog's behaviour? May it not be argued that the dog had become frightened by the bombing so close to the house only twelve hours previously and had decided to seek the safest place possible?

This argument certainly deserves consideration, but even if one accepted it as a reason for the dog's behaviour, it does not provide a complete answer for what took place that day. At the time of the incident the spaniel was nearly six years old and had been with the family all the years of the war, so bombing was nothing new. Anyone who has ever kept dogs, as I have, knows that a dog which has been accepted and treated as a member of the family stays with the family under all circumstances unless something exceptional is taking place or, as seems probable here, is about to take place.

Mr and Mrs Hume are archaeologists. Mr Hume's comment on the case is interesting:

The family had abandoned the shelter because it leaked and for years had slept in a table shelter in the house. But because of the dog's persistence they pumped it out and agreed to use it that night. They did, and the same night a flying bomb flattened the house. This, I think, is the clearest possible evidence of precognition on the part of the dog, but more interesting is the fact that the family (and the next door neighbour) agreed to spend the night in a damp shelter in the garden that they had not used in four years. It was not a rational thing to do, and I can imagine countless reasons why they should have ignored the dog. Is it possible that the communication was at a level beyond the senses, making the irrational reasonable? I suppose I mean beyond consciousness!

Mr Hume's argument goes to the heart of the matter. There were, as he said, countless reasons why the family should have ignored the dog but they did not.

Before we make up our minds about this case, we should consider the evidence for what has been called the *psi*-function in animals.

In *The Hidden Springs* (Little, Brown, 1974), Renée Haynes says that it is very difficult to estimate, appraise or define the working of *psi* in animals. There are three main reasons for this, she says. The first is that we know so little of their mode of consciousness; what they are aware of, and how they feel about it. The second reason is connected with the first. Animals have no means of precise communication with us. The third reason is that animals' senses are developed in other directions and degrees than ours, and that many of the sensory means of perception and communication natural to them are incomprehensible in terms of direct human experience. 'Scientific discovery, deduction and experiment have enabled us to have an intellectual knowledge of some of the occurrences of which they are immediately aware; but there may still be others of which we know nothing,' says Miss Haynes, who maintains that *psi* in domestic creatures should be examined from a slightly different angle from *psi* in totally wild ones:

> It will in fact be useful to bear in mind in all investigations of animal *psi* a general distinction between three sorts of animal group: those whose existence has no direct connexion with that of human beings such as ants, and the blind white fish of subterranean lakes; those which have a sort of symbiotic relationship with man, like bees, pigs, sheep, cattle and carrier pigeons; and domestic pets, dogs, cats, budgerigars, whose behaviour is modified and whose consciousness is probably extended and sensitized by daily assimilation into the human way of life.

Miss Haynes's remarks about the behaviour of domestic animals are, I believe, relevant to the incident of the dog Merry at Wimbledon.

Mr John Randall, in an article on recent experiments in animal psychology in *Journal* of the SPR for September 1972, says that there is a good deal of anecdotal evidence which suggests that animals display *psi* abilities in the absence of any intending human agent.

The most striking examples of apparent spontaneous *psi* in animals, Mr Randall states, are those where a dog or cat, left behind when the family moves to a distant home, somehow finds its way to them. One such case concerns Tony, a mongrel dog belonging to the Doolen family of Illinois. When the Doolens left Aurora for their new home in Lancing, Michigan, they gave Tony away, but six weeks later he appeared in Lancing and greeted Mr Doolen in the street. He was identified by the collar which Mr Doolen had bought for him in Aurora and which had had an extra hole cut in it to fit Tony's size. The animal seems to have '*psi*-trailed' his master over a distance of 120 miles as the crow flies, though, because Lake Michigan is interposed between the two towns, he would have had to travel further than this on the ground.

'There are quite a number of such cases on record,' says Mr Randall, 'and it does not seem possible to explain them in sensory terms, even if we postulate as yet undiscovered sensory mechanisms.'

Mr Randall gives details of experiments involving rats, goldfish and mice in which they seem to exhibit precognition.

In 1968 two French scientists reported one of the most ingenious and sophisticated *psi* experiments ever performed. A binary random number generator was used to apply electric shocks to one or other of the two halves of a cage in which a mouse was confined. The movements of the animal were automatically monitored by a photocell device. It was found that the mice were able to avoid going to that half of the cage which was about to receive the shock to an extent producing odds against chance of about 1,000 to 1. American researchers have successfully repeated the French work using random number generators of the type designed by Dr Helmut Schmidt and automatic punch-tape recording.

Now the time has come to sum up. It seems to me that if, on the evidence, we allow that precognition occurs among men, women and children at times, we must also allow that it may occur among animals. Although the case of the cocker spaniel Merry is old, going back thirty years, the circumstances were so dramatic and unusual that it is unlikely they would be distorted by memory. Mrs Hume, who observed the behaviour of the dog, impressed me as being a very good witness, and there is independent evidence for her account.

It could be argued by critics that it was a coincidence that on the night the Baines family and their neighbour moved into the garden shelter their home was destroyed by a bomb. The critics could also argue that it was just a coincidence that the dog, frightened by recent bombing, chose that particular day to keep on returning to the garden shelter again and again for the first time in four years. Thus we have coincidence added to coincidence. I feel it is more logical, in the circumstances, to attribute the dog's behaviour to precognition.

7 Death of a watchmaker

In the morning of 15 October 1968, Miss Crystal Rogers woke in Tilburg, Holland, with a feeling of heaviness and depression. She attributed this to the fact that she was leaving all her friends after a visit to England and going back the following day to India, where she runs a clinic for animals.

The previous night she had mentioned to her friend, the Baroness van Dedem Faure, that she wished she had been able to buy a small cheap watch to take back to her servant. The Baroness immediately replied, 'I know a watchmaker who will be able to sell you one. We can go there in the morning.'

Now that it was morning, Miss Rogers found that the funeral march kept on ringing in her head, so much so that she remarked on this to the Baroness and said, 'I hope no one has died.'

Miss Rogers wrote to me from India:

> An hour or so later we went down to the town and incidentally the watch shop, but just before reaching it we came upon a funeral procession with the bier just about to be carried into the church and the bell tolling. We carried on to the watch shop only to find it closed, as the proprietor had just died, and it was his funeral we had just witnessed.
>
> This story seems completely pointless, but on account of its oddness I have related it to you. The watch maker meant nothing to me as I had never met him or heard of him before.

Miss Rogers enclosed a letter from the Baroness confirming her account.

She said that this experience 'appears to be some form of precognition'. The feeling of 'heaviness and depression' and the strains of the funeral march which kept on ringing in her head made her wonder at first whether her plane would crash, and it was only later that she attributed her feeling to the possibility that someone had died or was going to die. There was nothing personal in this experience, any more than there was on a previous occasion when she was driving with her mother through the New Forest, nowhere near any town or village, and started humming the funeral march, just before turning a corner to meet a hearse followed by a funeral procession – 'not the sort of thing one expects to see, somehow, in the middle of the New Forest,' Miss Rogers remarked.

However, there are times when a feeling of depression does relate to a personal tragedy.

On 22 June 1963, Mr Ronald Prentice, Deputy Advertisement Director of *Investors Chronicle*, London, and his late wife, were happily awaiting the coming down of their son Roger from Christchurch, Oxford. It was the last day of his first year and also his sister's birthday. They had a late lunch and had prepared a very special strawberry tea, and awaited the return home of the boy and the arrival of very close friends to share the joy.

Mr Prentice wrote to me:

> At about 2 o'clock I walked into our garden and was looking northward through the roses when I was visibly stricken with an appalling grief and fear. My late wife was watching me through the window, saw this happening to me, and rushed to put her arms around me. She asked what was happening to me and I said that I had a feeling of the most dreadful impending tragedy. She comforted me as best as she could but I felt very low, but without any known reason. The premonition of disaster coincided with the approximate time of departure of my son from the university at around 2 o'clock. The local police came to my house at Dulwich and informed me that our son had been killed instantly in a road accident near Denham at about 2.30 p.m. The premonition therefore came at the time that he set out from Oxford to come home. Since then my first wife has also died. Her death came in 1969 after four years of bitter struggle with leukemia.

I corresponded with Mr Prentice, who is chairman of two of the social work bodies of The Society of Friends, about this case. He said that his son, who was an exhibitioner at Oxford and a brilliant scholar, was driving a Vespa scooter when he was killed. It was significant that Mr Prentice had never before felt such a warning of disaster.

This case, and that of Miss Rogers, bring to mind the comment of Professor C. D. Broad in his chapter on the notion of precognition in *Science and ESP* that 'Whatever may be the nature of the allegedly precognitive event, it does not usually carry with it, for the person in whom it occurs, any *explicit reference to the future*. That it was concerned with something still in the future is generally suspected only later, and often only after a certain event or state of affairs has occurred and has been noted and compared with it.'

I assume that Roger Prentice had no premonition of death or disaster when he set out from Oxford, although, of course, I cannot be sure about this. However, in certain cases such a premonition is felt. An example is as follows:

On the morning of 12 September 1969, we left our home in a suburb of Bristol at approximately 8.45 am, my husband Harold Thomas, aged 54, and myself Elizabeth Thomas, aged 46.[1]

He was an area supervisor for a London firm of structural steel manufacturers and his function was to inspect the various structures within the area. I occasionally accompanied him when he had to meet a colleague and we would lunch together. I had decided only the previous night to go on the trip to Evesham as I had been rather busy making jam and chutney.

The morning was overcast and there had been some rain. As we were travelling up the A38 *en route* to Gloucester at roughly 9.15 am, Harold held my hand in his and I exclaimed at the coldness of it which was most unusual as *I* and not *he* normally felt the cold.

A little later before we reached Gloucester he again held my hand in his, which was still very cold. I asked him why his hands were so cold and he replied, 'Fear.'

'Of what?' I asked, but he simply said, 'I don't know.'

This incident was utterly out of my husband's character as he was a most prosaic person, very down to earth and not given to imagining things. I felt a little disturbed at this revelation as he had said it with a little sort of laugh – half derisory almost, as if he were rather ashamed at such an admission.

However, we had by this time reached Tewkesbury through which we passed as slowly as traffic would allow to admire the beauty of the ancient buildings of which we were very fond. As we left the town *en route* to Evesham Harold said, 'We won't take the main

[1] Pseudonyms have been provided at the request of the lady who gave details of this very sad case.

road as the other is much prettier and you would enjoy it more.'

We then joined the Bredon Road and were rounding a left hand bend bordered by a very high hedge. Suddenly we were confronted by a very high wide vehicle coming in the opposite direction. Up to the very second of impact I thought we were going to avoid it. I heard my husband shout something – I am not certain what – and he furiously tried to steer the car away from a collision.

I don't remember anything more until the car was a wreck in the hedge. My husband was lying by my side. I put my arms around him and rested my head on his chest but there was no heart beat. I then became aware of the awful injuries he had suffered.

I was told later that death had been instantaneous at 9.56 am.

The interval between the time when Mrs Thomas first noticed the coldness of her husband's hand and the collision which resulted in his death was forty-one minutes. This coldness was certainly physical. Feelings of cold are frequently reported in cases where it seems that something of a paranormal nature is taking place and it is thought that in many such cases the feelings are subjective.

In the case I have just given, Mr Thomas had the premonition of disaster but not his wife. We will now consider a case in which both husband and wife had a strong feeling of impending disaster although they did not know the nature of it.

The account I will give below came from Mrs Elizabeth Jones, of Portmadoc, Caernarvonshire. She wrote to me because she had read my book *Frontiers of the Unknown*. Referring to the death of her husband, Griffith Emyr Jones, of Ty Newydd, Ceidio, near Pwllheli, on 4 September 1971, Mrs Jones said:

Six months ago my 27-years-old husband was killed in a car crash. For three weeks before his death I kept getting a strange feeling each time I started doing any gardening or tidying up on our 26 acre small-holding which we had only recently purchased. I could actually hear a voice saying, 'What do you want to do this for? You won't be here much longer.' I had a horrible, uncomfortable feeling each time, and I was restless all the time. Then about three o'clock one morning my husband woke me up and said 'I won't be here much longer. You'll see what I mean soon.' I told him plainly to shut up and go back to sleep and all he said was 'You'll see.'

On the Monday before he died [he was killed at 11.30 pm on the following Saturday] he rang my parents up and asked them to come and take me away for a short holiday. This was something he'd never done before. My parents came on the Tuesday and I went, but very reluctantly. Again I had this horrible feeling come over me, but I went. My husband rang me that night but I'd gone to bed and my mother didn't wake me to go to the phone. He didn't ring again.

At seven o'clock on the Sunday morning my parents told me that he had been killed in a crash at 11.30 the previous evening. He was a passenger in his own car.

I learned later from friends who had been with him that night that they hadn't seen him so happy and cheerful for a long time as he was that particular night. He had also been to see most of his friends during the last few days, friends he hadn't seen for some time. I'm sure when I think back to those last three weeks we both knew something was going to happen, and I realize now I was far more frightened than my husband. He seemed quite calm all the while and now I realize he even arranged for me not to be alone when I was told the news. This I think explains why he sent for my parents to take me away. I have sold the farm now and have started a new life for myself and our two children.

I asked Mrs Jones a number of questions, one of which was whether she was frightened by her husband's driving and whether this could make her fear he would be involved in an accident. Mrs Jones replied:

It was true that I was frightened by my husband's driving in the past because he drove very fast and had had several narrow escapes, but when we had the two children he became a very careful driver and no longer loved speed because he often used to comment on my own somewhat fast driving. As for his friend, his driving never bothered me, and I had been his passenger on several occasions.

However, as Mr Jones was not driving when the accident took place, the question of his skill as a driver does not really come into the case.

The voice she heard was an inward one, she said.

Mrs Jones's mother, Mrs Lucy Edwards, of Dolgellau, Merioneth, confirmed her daughter's account. 'She often expressed her fears to me and to her father long before her husband was killed,' she said.

Mrs Jones sent me two newspaper cuttings relating to the death of her husband.

The evidence in this case is good. There is no suggestion of a 'death wish' on the part of Mr Jones. According to Mrs Jones, her husband and his friend went out for a drink, and when it came to closing time, Mr Jones decided he had had over the limit to drive so he asked his friend to do so. Mrs Edwards gives independent evidence of her daughter's concern for her husband's safety, adding in one of her letters to me, 'I am utterly convinced that people who are soon to die have some kind of premonition.'

The voice Mrs Jones heard was an inward one, but in the case I will relate now the voice heard by a woman in Sydney, Australia, came from 'behind my right shoulder, but seemed to be speaking into my head, rather than my ear.' She wrote to me because she had read *Apparitions and Ghosts* and said, 'You can relate this incident if you wish, but please don't use my name or address (I've relatives in England) and I'm afraid that people who hear voices are sometimes regarded as a little eccentric, so it's often far better to forget the whole incident'.

Let us call her, therefore, Mrs Marsden. In 1953 she was one of a group of young girls who had worked together in an office, had all married, left work, and each had had a child. Mrs Marsden had arranged a reunion in the Botanical Gardens, Sydney, where they were to meet at an appointed time and have a picnic lunch.

I was very excited at the prospect of meeting my friends again, seeing their new babies and showing off my Pride and Joy. I had looked forward to this day for weeks, as I now had an additional piece of news – I was two months pregnant. Life was wonderful.

I can still vividly recall standing at my front door all ready to depart, son in his pusher at my feet. I was mentally checking if I had everything: were the windows shut? was the back door locked? Whilst my mind was occupied with remembering that I had turned the key I was startled by a voice, quite loud, behind my right shoulder, but seemed to be speaking into my head rather than my ear. It said 'What would you rather, the day out or the baby?' I was dumbstruck, to say the least. The first thought that came to my mind was to stay at home. Then I wondered what I would say. [If I said] 'a voice told me' they'd think me mad. I couldn't say I was taken ill: I had been talking to one of them on the phone half an hour earlier. I couldn't ring any of them now, anyway – they'd all left home by now. They would be waiting for me, and, after all, hadn't I been the one to arrange the whole picnic?

I dismissed the voice and left.

The trip into Sydney went well until I left the train at St James's station. There is a flight of stairs from underground level to the roadway, and on lifting the pusher with my weighty son on board up a difficult step I felt a sickening lurch in my stomach. I didn't enjoy the day at all, as I had cramps in my stomach all day. Later that night, I'm sad to relate, I had a miscarriage.

I had some doubts at first about including this case in a chapter giving accounts of deaths but decided to do so because it may be regarded as referring to the death of an unborn child.

The information which came to Mrs Marsden in auditory form obviously related to the risk she ran if she went on an excursion pushing a heavy baby in a form of carriage. Such information can come through in various ways. In his book *Foreknowledge*, H. F. Saltmarsh gives details of a strange experience by Lady Craik, daughter of Dame Edith Lyttelton. She was once on the point of crossing Victoria Street, London, in front of a stationary bus, when she felt a strong hand on her shoulder which pulled her back sharply. At the same time a motor-cycle swerved past the bus, going very fast between it and the refuge. She turned to thank whoever had saved her, but to her surprise there was no one within reach. Mr Saltmarsh comments that 'Here the event was practically simultaneous with the warning *and it seems probable that the subliminal mind of Lady Craik was aware of the threatened danger and conveyed the warning to the normal consciousness by means of a tactile hallucination*' (my italics).

I agree with Mr Saltmarsh's interpretation. In Mrs Marsden's case it seems probable that her subliminal mind was aware of the threatened danger to her unborn child if she went on the excursion and conveyed the warning to the normal consciousness by means of an auditory hallucination.

Another example of a warning being conveyed by a tactile hallucination was given to me by Mrs Janet Wells (pseudonym), of Dronfield, near Sheffield. Her little girl was six months old when she had the experience:

I was awoken in the early hours of the morning by a violent shaking of the shoulders and pressure on my back. Even when awake fully I could still feel it. My first thought was my baby and I rushed into her room, where she was lying in her cot with all the bedcovers tucked right over her head, and she was laid on them. I am sure if I had not gone into her room she would have suffocated.

Mrs Amelia Adamson, of Edgware, Middlesex, had returned from a visit to her parents in November 1958, and was asleep when the telephone rang downstairs at 1.30 a.m. Her husband answered it, came up to her bedroom and said, 'Your mother has just passed away.'

Mrs Adamson said to me in her letter:

As he told me the dream I had just had came back to me. I dreamed my mother was standing by an open grave. She turned to me and pointed down and I walked slowly towards her looking down. I saw a coffin with my father's name in gold lettering: 'In loving memory of James John Sutton.'

A month later my father died. He couldn't have lived long without her. When we were at the graveside I looked down and saw the exact coffin and gold lettering as I had seen in my dream.

I think my mother gave me that message just as she passed away.

Mrs Adamson's daughter, Mrs Margaret Difford, of Stanmore, Middlesex, confirmed that she had been told by her mother about the dream before Mr Sutton's death. 'I remember how strange it was that she should have had this dream just as her mother had died,' she said. 'Then when her father died it all seemed to make sense.'

An obvious question to be addressed to Mrs Adamson was the state of her father's health at the time.

'My father wasn't ill at the time of her death and I am sure had she lived he would have lived for many more years,' she replied. 'He had suffered from bronchitis for many years but that had been due to the nature of his work.'

Mr Sutton died on 1 January 1959, and is buried in Neasden Cemetery.

On the night of 12 February 1956, Mrs Winifred Eagle, of Holland Road, East Ham, London, had just finished grooming her dog and was going out to empty the water when she glanced up the hall and saw by the front door the shadow of her sister's son, Thomas Avery.

'I felt cold and shaky at the same time,' said Mrs Eagle. 'I then ran upstairs and told my husband that I had seen Tommy by the door. Well, the next night the front [door] bell rang at the same time. Wondering who it could be so late [I found] on opening the door that it was Tommy. He had come to tell me that his mother (my sister) had died suddenly. Could this be an apparition?'

I corresponded with Mrs Eagle about this case. She said that her sister's name was Beatrice Avery and that she had died suddenly on 13 February 1956. The glass of the door was high up and frosted, the hall was dark and there was a street lamp on the opposite side of the road. It was the light of this lamp that reflected into the hall and showed the shadow of her nephew, who was aged twenty-two at the time. The only people in the house at the time were her husband and herself. She woke her husband up and told him what she had seen.

Mr Eagle sent me the following statement: 'This is to confirm that my wife did wake me and that she did tell me that she had seen a shadow or shape of our nephew (Tommy). The following night he did call and told us of his mother's sudden death the previous day.' [Mr Eagle obviously means the same day. I obtained a copy of the death certificate of Mrs Beatrice Avery, of 50A Dryden Close, Ilford, Essex, aged 59, of coronary thrombosis and angina pectoris, on 13 February 1956. Her son T., presumably Thomas, Avery was present at the death.]

The testimony of Thomas Avery would obviously help in this case. At the time of his mother's death he was serving in the Royal Air Force and was stationed in Essex. As he is now living in Kentucky in the United States, and does not write often, Mrs Eagle did not think she could get a statement from him on my behalf. I wondered whether he had come physically to the house on the night when Mrs Eagle first saw him, but if he had he would obviously have rung the front door bell: the time was only 10.30 p.m.

In the circumstances it seems that one must draw the conclusion that Mrs Eagle saw, twenty-four hours in advance of his actual arrival, the figure of her nephew who was to bring the news of her sister's death.

8 A surgeon's experience

On a Saturday evening in 1964, a distinguished surgeon whom I will call Mr Donald Wilson – this is not his real name – had a dream in which he was seeing patients in his consulting room on the following Monday morning, and the first patient was a woman who had a large discoloured patch on her right buttock.

He could not see the woman's face nor the whole of her body: the dream was focused on her buttocks. He had never before dreamt of a patient, certainly not one whom he had not seen before. Naturally, he awaited the Monday morning surgery with more than usual interest. The first patient shown to him was a nurse.

'So much for my dream,' the surgeon thought. The nurse was examined and left. Later he discovered that she had been added to the list only that morning and had been put at the top of it so that she could return to her duties. The next patient was a woman who had not been to his surgery before.

When she was lying on the examination couch on her left side, he noticed a large discoloured tumour, about one and a half inches long by an inch wide, on her right buttock.

He was startled by this and even more startled by the position of the lesion.

'But it's two inches lower than I thought it was!' he exclaimed aloud, probably to the astonishment of the woman, who had not come to him for his advice on this patch of discoloured skin.

'If I had not had the dream, I would have left this tumour where it was,' Mr Wilson told me. 'But because of the dream I thought, "This is too significant not to do anything about it." '

Two days later the tumour was removed and on examination proved to be malignant.

'It is what is known to doctors as an "*in situ* lesion" and could have broken out at any time,' Mr Wilson explained. 'If it had not been removed the woman would have died.'

It was highly unusual for a pigmented tumour of this type to be on the buttocks, Mr Wilson said. He had not seen one in this position before.

The surgeon was able to make another fortunate intervention in a case involving a woman. This time it was one whom he knew socially as well as professionally. The incident took place in 1955.

With his wife, he had been invited to a cocktail party. At the time he was very tired and in pain from two slipped discs, and he knew that the worst thing he could do was to stand up for any length of time. However, he overcame his reluctance to go to the party because he thought it was his duty to do so. Three times during the party he felt he must leave but some inner compulsion prevented him. Then, across the long room, he caught the eye of a woman he knew: he had helped to bring her three children into the world. At that moment he felt that he must speak to her. As he approached the woman she raised her glass in her left hand and said, 'Your very good health, Donald.'

The surgeon returned the greeting and, knowing that his friend was right-handed, asked 'Do you usually hold your glass in your left hand?'

'No, I don't,' she replied.

If the woman had not raised the glass in her left hand, the sleeve of her frock would not have slipped back to reveal a small tumour above the wrist, 'as black as could be', in the surgeon's own words when I interviewed him.

In reply to inquiries the woman said that the tumour had been growing darker in colour and that her children, who were then dependent on her, had remarked on this.

Mr Wilson, realizing the significance of the darkening colour of the tumour – this could be an indication that it was becoming malignant – asked the woman to see him at the hospital the following morning. The tumour was then removed and examination proved it to be malignant.

'If the operation had not been carried out she would have been dead in two years', Mr Wilson said. 'Her children needed her desperately then.' He felt there had been purpose in his reluctant attendance at that party.

I first came across these two cases in Dr Arthur Guirdham's book *Obsession* (Neville Spearman, 1972). Mr Wilson kindly agreed to see me. He is a man in his early sixties and of Highland Scottish descent. Although he was not born in South Africa, he spent part of his boyhood there. When he was seven he was in delicate health and because of this was kept in bed for six months. During this period, when he was living at an altitude of 6,000 feet, he had a series of dreams of English ancestral homes. One dream in particular stayed in his mind. It was of a house sited dramatically on solid rock with a great sweep of lawn below on which cypresses grew. During the war he served as a medical officer in the British Army. Changes of billet were frequent and some of these took him to stately homes of the type he had seen in his boyhood dreams. But it was with a sense of shock, when he went to join a field ambulance unit in Sussex, that he turned a corner and saw the house he had remembered from his dreams, built on a rock and with cypresses dotted on the lawn.

There was no doubt, he told me, that it was the same house: Leyswood, near Groombridge.

Since Mr Wilson was there, the house, which was built in 1869, has been mostly pulled down and, 'alas, only survives as a fragment,' according to Ian Nairn and Nikolaus Pevsner in their volume on Sussex in the series *The Buildings of England* (Penguin, 1965). They add, 'The disappearance of this most picturesque, even if still a little melodramatic mansion, is a shame.'

They describe the house as being built 'on a wild terrace of natural rocks.'

When I called on Mr Wilson in early December, 1972, he told me of an incident when, instead of taking the usual turning to his home after leaving the hospital where he is a consultant, he found himself driving to another part of the town, although he had not intended to go that way. He could have turned back but decided to continue with his drive. Remembering that a friend who had recently had an operation lived in that vicinity, he thought he would make a call to inquire about his progress: it was a social call because the man was not his patient. His friend was so unwell that he asked about his treatment. The upshot of this unscheduled call was that he rang the doctor who was in charge of the case and, describing the deterioration in the condition of his friend, indicated that he was not responding to treatment. As a result the treatment was changed and his friend's health began to improve. Here again, as in the case of the cocktail party, Mr Wilson felt that there was a purpose behind his presence at a particular spot where someone was in need of help.

Mr Wilson's experience of seeing, with a sense of shock as an adult, the house of his childhood dreams, is paralleled by another precognitive dream of childhood related in the life of Sir Lewis Namier, the historian, by his wife (Oxford, 1971).

Lady Namier, who is a member of the SPR, describing a flight from Amsterdam with her husband, said:

> On our return to England I shared with him, as a matter of course, a sudden visual impression that had whisked me back to early childhood . . . We came over London after dark. Reclining by a window with L. between me and the gangway, I was wafted into a long since forgotten mood and state. As a child I had often flown in a recurrent dream, reclining in what I took to be a railway carriage without compartments and with someone on my right of whom I was cosily aware but whom I could never identify. I always woke after I had been looking out of a window on my left, down on to an unforgettable pattern of lights – red, green, blue, yellow, white. And there it was drifting below me. When it had gone I spoke. L. having often been struck by fleeting, but unmistakably substantiated, flashes of foreknowledge, had never speculated about their nature, not being equipped to do so usefully. But he had every time felt the event reinforce a scale of values that bolstered up his will to live. My communicated foreknowledge was helping him to return . . . refreshed . . . to battle. . . .

We may now turn to a precognitive dream about a house rather more specific than Mr Wilson's. In Dame Edith Lyttelton's *Some Cases of Prediction*, she tells how, in 1928, when Mr R. B. Calder was appointed headmaster of the Holmforth Secondary School, Yorkshire, his wife, who had never been to Yorkshire, dreamed at their home in Middlesex of an old house built of grey stone, situated in a lovely valley through which ran a shallow stream of black-looking water. Their house-hunting led them to the very place she had seen in her dream. The house was at Honley, three miles from Holmforth. The stream was frequently discoloured from the waste products of the neighbouring dye works. Only one detail was lacking. In Mrs Calder's dream she had seen that half of the house appeared to be occupied and outside the house was a barrel being used as a dog kennel for a black retriever. A year or so later new tenants arrived and Mrs Calder's dream was recalled to her very vividly when they brought with them a black Labrador retriever and placed a barrel by the door for its use.

On 19 December 1930, Mr Calder was appointed headmaster of the Goole Grammar School. Mrs Calder had never seen Goole nor had she been in this part of Yorkshire. On 28 December she dreamed of a dark red house vaguely square standing on a corner of two streets. There was a fence over which she could see a low flat garden. She described the house to her husband the following morning and said she felt convinced they would have to live in it, although she was depressed at the prospect of doing so. She also told her husband that, in her dream, Mr C. J. Forth, the retiring headmaster, and the two of them tried a front garden gate but failing to open it they walked down the side road and looked over a low fence into the garden. On 31 December Mr and Mrs Calder visited Goole to find a new house and after a long time they began to despair of finding anything suitable. At last Mr Forth took them to the house which Mrs Calder had seen in her dream. They failed to open the front garden gate, and walked down the side road to look over the low fence into the garden, just as Mrs Calder had forecast in her dream.

Entries in Mrs Calder's diary, which she had kept for some years, confirmed these facts.

Mrs Calder wrote to Dame Edith to say:

> Several of my friends at Honley had heard about my 'seeing' my house there before moving – and when we knew we were to move to Goole they often asked if I had 'seen' our future residence. Then when I actually did so – and was able to give details – they were sceptically interested until they were convinced by our actually finding and occupying the actual house.

Mrs Calder also had precognitive experiences as a child but did not give details of these as she had no verification for them.

One of the best examples of precognition concerning a house is the celebrated Gordon Davis case. The information came at a séance at which the medium was Mrs Blanche Cooper and the sitter Dr S. G. Soal, who was a lecturer in mathematics in London University. Dr Soal published the results of his sittings with Mrs Cooper in the *Proceedings* of the SPR in 1926.

Mrs Cooper was a direct voice medium and at a sitting on 4 January 1922, a voice said that it was 'Gordon Davis from R-R-Roch –'. Soal recognized this at once as the name of an old school friend from Rochford who, he believed, had been killed in the war. He asked the voice for proof of identity and the supposed Gordon Davis proceeded to refer to incidents in the past that were clearly recognizable to Dr Soal.

The next sitting was held five days later and the voice gave further snatches of information purporting to come from Gordon Davis. There were several references to his house and its contents: 'Something about a funny dark tunnel . . . to do with his house. . . . There're five or six steps and a half.' The house was said to be 'joined up to some others – don't think it's a proper street – like half a street . . . get the letter "E". There's something right in front of his house – not a veranda – something that's not in front of the other houses.' Inside the house there was said to be 'a very large mirror and lots of pictures . . . all scenes . . . glorious mountains and the sea . . . some vases . . . very big ones with funny saucers – downstairs there're two funny brass candlesticks . . . on a shelf . . . black dickie bird . . . on the piano. There's a woman . . . and a little boy . . . fond of the country . . . think it's his wife.'

Dr Soal kept careful notes, signed, dated and witnessed, of these sittings. It was not until February 1925, three years after the sittings with Mrs Cooper, that Dr Soal heard indirectly that Gordon Davis was still alive and was living in Southend. On 8 April that year Dr Soal went to see Mr Davis. He was living at 54 Eastern Esplanade (the *E*s). Six steps led up to the front door, but the lowest of these was only a thin slab ('five or six steps and a half'). It was a terraced house, joined on either side to its neighbours in the same block, and it faced the sea. There were no houses on the other side ('half a street'). A tunnel between each pair of front doors in the block led from the street to the back garden. Opposite the house, and in this sense in front of it, but on the other side of the street, was a seaside shelter. Inside the house, in the drawing-room, was one very large mirror above the mantelpiece, five very large vases, two saucer-shaped china plaques, seven pictures, every one of scenery, with mountains or sea in six of them. A small ornament in the form of a kingfisher, on a black pedestal, stood on the piano. On the mantelpiece in the dining-room, which was downstairs, stood two brass candlesticks, the only ones in the house. Mr Davis had a wife and one child, a boy of five.

Commenting on this case in his book *Psychical Research Today*, Dr D. J. West said:

> The medium was correct, or very nearly so, in every statement made, an extremely unlikely thing to happen by pure chance. The strangest fact of all, however, was that it was not until the end of 1922, nearly a year after the sittings with Mrs Cooper, that Gordon Davis moved into the house in Eastern Esplanade. He inspected the house for the first time on 6 January, just three days before the sitting. If it was from the mind of Gordon Davis that the medium derived her information, he must have had the house prominently in his thoughts at the time, but the interior ornamentation so well described by the medium was not planned in advance. Indeed it came about largely fortuitously. The Gordon Davis incident strongly suggests that the medium used her ESP faculty to foretell the future – precognition.

Professor C. W. K. Mundle, in his presidential address to the SPR in 1972 (published in the *Proceedings* for January 1973, under the heading of 'Strange Facts in Search of a Theory'), says:

> Some of Mrs Cooper's statements seemed to involve precognition, since they described some later contents of the Gordon Davis home, e.g. pictures of the sea which Gordon Davis acquired in 1924 and the 'dickie bird' on the piano. But presumably her ESP would not have become focused upon such things unless she had formed some telepathic rapport with Gordon Davis, mediated by telepathy with Soal. A different interpretation is, however, possible, i.e. that Soal did the precognizing and Mrs Cooper got the information by telepathy from Soal.

This chapter is headed 'A surgeon's experience', and although the section on houses was necessary because of Mr Wilson's precognitive experience of seeing Leyswood, it is time for us to return to medical matters. Admiral Angelos Tanagras, the former Health Officer of the Greek Royal Navy, whose book *Le Destin et La Chance* is mentioned in my introduction, quotes there a case dating back to November 1932, in which Mr P. Kapsis, a journalist, was at Loutraki (a watering place near Corinth) with Mr Athanatos, editor of the Athens newspaper *L'Homme Libre,* planning a trip to Mycene. After playing a little roulette at the Casino, Mr Kapsis made himself comfortable in an armchair, and then, although not asleep, he thought he suddenly heard the voice of his son John, aged four, who was in Athens, calling out to him insistently, 'Daddy, come, please come.'

Mr Kapsis was so impressed by the hallucination that after telling his story to Mr Athanatos he immediately took his car and returned to Athens, where he arrived at five o'clock the following morning. He found his family in excellent health, and with a sceptical smile he recalled his anxious premonition and spoke of the faith which people generally have in such phenomena. He went to bed in good spirits, but about eleven o'clock his wife awoke him, very worried. Young John had just had a haemorrhage of the kidneys, and acute nephritis had suddenly set in.

Admiral Tanagras's comment on this is interesting. He says, 'Mr Kapsis, who had psychic qualities, unconsciously sensed, by means of clairvoyance, the disease which was developing in the organism of his child, and his brain symbolized the feeling by means of an acoustical hallucination.'

The Admiral maintained that a large number of premonitions can be explained by clairvoyance, an example of this being premonition of a disease which has not yet appeared but the germs of which already exist in the organism.

He quotes a case provided by Mr C. Logothetis, a professor at the University of Athens:

> When I was young I had a dream in which I saw my small cousin Pan Tsaoussidis drowning in a river, in spite of the desperate efforts of my father to save him. Being very affected by this, I rushed to tell my grandmother about my dream. She said that it was bad – a very bad omen. Three days later the little boy, who had enjoyed perfect health, was struck down by meningitis, of which he died a week later.

Admiral Tanagras comments: 'This professor, who had psychic powers, had a subconscious presentiment of the meningitis germs which were developing in his cousin, and his brain symbolized the fatal outcome as death in a river. This presentiment, therefore, is an example of clairvoyance.'

Clairvoyance is a possible explanation of the strange case of a young man with his leg in plaster reported by Dr Arthur Guirdham.

A sister in a hospital ward doing the rounds with the registrar before the arrival of the consultant, was worried about the state of the leg of a young man who had suffered a compound fracture in a motor-cycle accident. The leg was in plaster and she asked the registrar to remove the plaster so that the leg could be examined. The registrar, who had set the fracture, was unwilling to do this because he felt it would not serve any useful purpose. When the consultant surgeon arrived, the sister implored him to remove the plaster and examine the leg, and to humour her, as he could see she was upset, he agreed to do so. It was then discovered that gas gangrene had set in. The leg was amputated. But for the sister's insistence that the leg should be examined immediately the young man would have died.

The presence of a serious abnormal lesion such as a tumour or bad abscess caused this sister to get a characteristic tremor of her hands from the tips of her fingers to her elbow 'like a dowser's tremor,' Dr Guirdham remarked to me. She also had many 'hunches' about when people were going to become seriously ill. The special capacity of her fingers was a separate gift.

Dr Louisa E. Rhine discusses in *ESP in Life and Lab* a number of precognitive experiences reported by nurses, and comments: 'The liberal number of ESP experiences from nurses suggests that theirs is a profession that either creates situations made to order for ESP or else a subtle selection of personality types occurs with nurses so that they tend to have ESP experiences more often than the average.'

I have often found it difficult to obtain corroborative evidence of experiences occurring in hospitals reported to me, since those who could give this evidence apparently feel that they are unable to do so because of medical ethics. The account that now appears comes from a correspondent who has reported other cases which I have been able to verify. I will give her the pseudonym of Mrs Mathieson. A few years ago she took a job in a leading London teaching hospital.

This will sound morbid, I am afraid, but I would always know when a patient would die, although all appeared to be going well and the doctors pleased and confident. I could see what I can only describe as a kind of fuzzy white aura round the patient's body. One old lady died suddenly in the middle of eating her lunch. I kept looking at her from my desk and finally told the staff nurse. 'Nonsense!', she said. 'Look at her. She's doing fine!' Five minutes later she died with knife and fork in hand. One beautiful young girl called Janet (pseudonym), only 26 years old, had made a remarkable recovery from a cancer operation. She had to go home the next day. That morning I woke feeling very sad and depressed and thought 'I must take Janet some roses from the garden.' On reaching my hospital ward I saw Janet all ready and dressed, and her young husband picking up her suitcases. A sort of shock went through me and I said to the sister, who had remarked wasn't it wonderful how well she had become, 'but Sister, Janet will never leave this hospital!' The sister gave me a strange look (I think she had doubts about my mental state!). I walked up to Janet, kissed her, and said 'Some roses for your journey!' She smiled her thanks, looked at me right in the eyes as though she and I knew her secret, and suddenly collapsed and fell back on the bed. She was dead. 'How did you know?', the sister asked me afterwards. I had to confess I didn't know *how* – I just did. Janet, by the way, had no aura round her. . . .

I wrote to the sister concerned, stating that her name and that of the hospital would not be revealed, but did not receive a reply. I feel that if Mrs Mathieson's story had been a fabrication I would have been told to ignore it but, as I have indicated, I have found her to be a reliable person and one possessing unusual powers. Possibly the sister felt that on ethical grounds she could not discuss matters affecting a patient.

9 Various experiences

A librarian in Sarasota, Florida, Mrs Elizabeth Gould Davis, who had read my book *Frontiers of the Unknown*, was so impressed by the account of the experiences of the late Lady Rhys Williams, whose precognitive gifts included 'hearing' reports in advance on the radio and 'reading' something in a newspaper before the notice actually appeared, that she decided to send me an account of a very strange experience of her own for which there was corroborative evidence.

It concerned the death of William C. Bullitt, adviser to Presidents Wilson and Roosevelt, former US Ambassador to Moscow and to France, and author of several books, at Neuilly, France, on 15 February 1967.

Mrs Davis told two other librarians about Bullitt's death before it actually occurred.

Let us hear Mrs Davis's story in her own words.

I must say, first, that I have never had any reason to have been interested in Bullitt, and that as a matter of fact my knowledge of him and his life was extremely hazy. I am a librarian, and in the month of February 1967 prior to Friday the 11th his book on Woodrow Wilson was received at the library where I am employed. I said casually, on seeing the book in an incoming shipment, 'Here's the Bullitt book on Wilson. He died the other day, you know, in France.' My co-worker said 'Oh, where did you hear that?' I replied 'On the radio news, or TV, or maybe I read it in the paper. I've forgotten now. But he died suddenly in France, apparently.' 'Well, I hadn't heard,' she remarked and turned to other matters. On the following Friday, 11 February 1967, a fellow librarian from another city was visiting me here for the week-end, and, as usual, we discussed the new books. The Bullitt book came up and I said something to her to the effect that she could 'close his dates' on the catalogue cards because he had died recently *in France*. She too was surprised (but not terribly excited) by the news, only because she had missed the item.

On Sunday 13 February this friend returned to her own home. On Tuesday evening 15 February I turned on the TV to the evening news as usual. About midway through the broadcast Mr Huntley, the newscaster, announced that ex-Ambassador William Bullitt had died *that day*, suddenly, *in France*!

I decided that Huntley must have gotten hold of an old script by error and so listened to the CBS news following. Again it was announced that Bullitt had died suddenly that day *in France*. Still I was puzzled by the rehashing of this old news and worried about it until the morning papers arrived on 16 February. There, datelined France, was the news of Bullitt's death on the day before. . . .

I mentioned the discrepancy to my co-worker above mentioned and she said 'You must have been having one of your ESP attacks.' That evening my house guest of the previous week-end called me long distance to find out what was going on. 'Bullitt died yesterday,' she said, 'not last week. You must have dreamed it.'

But I did not dream it. I either heard it on a news broadcast or read it in the paper over a week before it happened. The oddest thing about it is that it concerned a person in whom I had absolutely no interest, and who as far as I knew could well have been dead for years before that February 1967. How does one account for this? And why the persistent detail about *France*? And if it was intended as a warning message, why did it come to *me*?

A hand-written statement in support of this was signed by Elizabeth G. Davis (dated 16 February 1967) and Cody H. Allen. Mrs Allen is reference librarian at the Leon County Public Library, Tallahassee, Florida.

Mrs Davis's letter was dated 15 March 1970. The 'co-worker' she mentioned is Mrs Charles A. Service, Librarian-in-Chief of the Sarasota Public Library. In a letter dated 11 June 1970, she said:

In early February of 1967 she (Mrs Davis) and I were checking in a shipment of new books when Mrs Davis remarked that William Bullitt had recently died 'in France'. Not having heard this news myself I asked Mrs Davis where she had learned it. She could not remember that, but assumed she had heard it on the television news. This could not have occurred later than 9 February – Thursday – as Mrs Davis was off from Friday to Monday that week. On Wednesday 15 February the news was broadcast on television in the evening that William Bullitt had died that day 'in France'.

This is a strong case when the supporting evidence for Mrs Davis's experience is taken into consideration. Mrs Davis, who is now a writer and no longer works in the library, said she had received the information about Bullitt's death over a week before it occurred. Mrs Service is not certain of the time but puts it at least six days before the announcement of the death on television. It is a comparatively recent case. Mrs Davis made a note of the experience at the time, dated it, and Mrs Allen added her signature to the account. It is not clear how Mrs Davis gained the information: she just knew, in advance, that Bullitt was dead.

Unless we assume that the three librarians concocted a story to deceive me, Mrs Davis's story should be accepted. If a person holding strong critical views still maintains doubts about the truth of this account, may we not assume that three librarians would concoct something more dramatic than the death of an elderly and retired diplomat if they wanted to make an impression with a story on ESP? I see no reason to doubt the honesty of Mrs Davis and the two witnesses who have vouched for her story.

Another strong case for which supporting evidence is available came from Australia. Names have been changed or withheld at the request of the woman who had this experience because she does not want her child questioned at school. Let us call her Mrs Marshall and the child Helen.

At 10 a.m. on 2 June 1971, Mrs Marshall was cleaning her young daughter's bedroom floor in a town in New South Wales when 'a loud voice near my head said "Helen has hurt her leg." Then saw vision, headmaster bringing her home in car from school. Told myself "Don't be silly." Odd, because headmaster did bring Helen home, in same car seen in vision, and she had hurt her leg. Time approximately 12.50 p.m. Strange because the accident had happened at about 12.30 p.m. Saw this before accident had even occurred.'

Mrs Marshall went to see her next door neighbour. I have had a letter from this neighbour in which she says:

Mrs Marshall did say she was worried about Helen as she felt she had been hurt in some way at school. In fact I recall she even mentioned she had seen a vision that morning concerning Helen being brought home and spoke about other similar experiences. . . . As far as actual words and time distance factors are concerned I cannot be absolutely sure, as it is quite some time since the incident occurred. One thing of which I can be very sure is our conversation took place before Helen was brought home, and although I cannot swear to it I feel it was an hour or so before.

Mrs Marshall rang the records department at the hospital where Helen, then aged nine, had her leg treated to check certain facts. Examination had revealed that no bones were broken, but there was a nasty swelling on the bone and she was given a tetanus injection.

In later correspondence Mrs Marshall amended the time when Helen was brought home to approximately 1.40 p.m.

I wrote to the headmaster concerned, outlined the details given to me by Mrs Marshall, and asked if he could confirm them, which he did.

This is an interesting case because it involved clairvoyance (the vision of the headmaster bringing the child home in his car) and an auditory hallucination. It is noteworthy that in one of her early letters to me Mrs Marshall related an incident in which she heard her name called 'loudly and with urgency. Stopped pegging washing on line, ran to see who was calling. No one there. Puzzled.' She seems to be subject to auditory hallucinations, but the accounts of her experiences also include clairvoyance and telepathy ('I have what I believe to be numerous telepathic messages from my children. All have been correct information and conveyed to me in photographic form'). Precognition was, of course, involved in the incident involving Helen's accident. It seems to me that these various incidents prove very clearly that Mrs Marshall's experiences are different manifestations of the same faculty, ESP.

We have to decide in this case, as we did in the Florida one, whether what has been related here is the result of collusion between the headmaster, Mrs Marshall and her neighbour, or whether it happened more or less as related. It is a comparatively recent case and there is no reason to assume that distance in time has blurred recollection of events. I have addressed a number of letters to Mrs Marshall to clarify details and she gives every indication of being an honest witness. I believe, on the basis of the supporting evidence and also on Mrs Marshall's own testimony, that she has given a truthful account of a very strange incident.

A report of a precognitive experience which came from Mrs Cynthia Aspinall of Dulwich Village, London, contained some interesting features and is a good example of how impressions which rise from the subconscious may be wrongly interpreted.

In the early morning of 12 August 1970, Mr and Mrs Aspinall drove their younger daughter Gillian to a rendezvous at Norbiton Junction to see her off on a coach tour with friends to Yugoslavia. It was a beautiful summer morning and the time was 6.30.

We, and she, were being happy about this trip, and had no qualms about it as we waved her goodbye until the coach was out of sight. Then just as my husband was about to put the car in gear for our homeward journey I felt the most terrible pain right through my body, especially in the area of my ribs. Covered my face with my hands, trying in vain to stifle an uncontrollable scream. My husband, more amazed than alarmed, asked what was wrong. I said nothing about the pain but only stated that I could see shattered glass all over the road. . . . My husband said calmly that I mustn't be too anxious about Gillian. She was perfectly safe, and on her way to a wonderful holiday. I recovered and we drove slowly away on our way home. It was quiet, the streets empty of traffic, so we decided to go into Richmond Park to watch the sun which was rising in a beautiful red glow. In seconds, a youth driving a sports car (as we found out later) . . . crashed us sideways on and we landed against a brick wall. I blacked out, and when I opened my eyes all I could see from the stretcher on which I was lying, covered in blankets, was a sea of broken glass, shining and glittering in the sun – just as I had 'seen' before – and I could hardly speak for pain. At the hospital it was found I had four broken ribs, severe shock, and various minor injuries. My husband was unhurt. The car was a write-off.

I asked for a letter in confirmation of this account and for additional details from Mrs Aspinall's husband, Mr Kenneth Aspinall. He said that the time the coach left was about 6.45 a.m. 'Before setting off to drive back home to Dulwich I remember my wife going very quiet and then saying to me something like:

"Ken, I can see glass, broken glass, on the ground. . . ." I naturally assumed that she was thinking of Gillian's long coach journey and, as she is a sensitive person and quite often has such feelings, was having fears or presentiments about a possible accident.'

He put the time of the accident at 7 a.m. or just afterwards. 'The cause of the accident was the very bright, rising sun against which I was driving and which caused me to fail to see traffic lights at the road junction and to go across when the lights had apparently just turned red. We were struck in the middle of the crossing by a light sports car, as a result of which our car was sent off course and – ironically – collided with the traffic light control box on the left hand opposite side of the road, shattering it and its glass as well as my car.'

Mr Aspinall was subsequently charged with 'driving without due care and attention', and although he defended the case with the help of a barrister provided by his insurance company, was fined £15 plus costs and an endorsement.

It will be noted that the time between Mrs Aspinall's experience of 'seeing' glass on the road and the accident was fifteen minutes or possibly a minute or two more. Mr Aspinall interpreted the experience as referring to their daughter but it applied, in fact, to them. It is most interesting, and unusual, that Mrs Aspinall experienced the physical injuries which were the result of the accident *in advance*, but recovered only to experience them all over again when the accident occurred.

An adequate study still remains to be made on whether psychical gifts may be inherited. Mrs Aspinall has given me details of many strange experiences she has had and adds:

I may mention I come from a family of 'psychics'. My grandfather was a friend of Sir Oliver Lodge, and he, my grandfather, was a clergyman of absolute honesty. My mother was a most practical sensible woman, although very sensitive, and we were brought up with her remarkable 'second sight' as we called it, with enough experiences to write a book. But she was totally against any form of Spiritualism or occult practices, believing if apparitions appear or unexplainable situations they must be spontaneous and never sought. I seem to have inherited her gift (if one can call it that), and from the age of nine (my first, which I recall vividly) I have seen and inwardly been aware of many strange things. . . .

Mr Aspinall's confirmation that his wife had told him *before* the accident to their car occurred that she had 'seen' broken glass on the ground makes this case one of good evidential value.

Another case which hinges on how impressions may be interpreted was sent to me by the Rev. Alan Taylor, The Vicarage, Morton, Gainsborough, Lincolnshire. Mr Taylor, who is Countryside Officer for the Diocese of Lincoln, wrote in December 1972:

I was sitting in my car cleaning the dashboard and windscreen on a summer afternoon. The car was in the drive of the country vicarage [Hainton, Lincolnshire] where we lived at the time (about five years ago). I was sitting with my back to the road.

As I worked I began to reminisce about a man I had known in the Air Force when we were ground crew of the same squadron. This man, whose name was Boor [pseudonym], a curious surname and therefore remembered when others had been forgotten, was a bulky individual with heavy features. He was not a close friend but I remembered that he wore a denim or twill jacket and trousers to work in rather than the overalls which were standard issue. I never knew where he acquired these garments which were battered representatives of those worn by servicemen in tropical countries. After a while my thoughts moved on to other matters.

A few minutes later there was a tap at the car window and I was staggered to see what appeared to be the same man standing on the drive, with whom I had had no contact for twenty years.

However, after a momentary shock I realized that this was not the man of whom I had been thinking. It was another man, Anthony Grant [pseudonym], who had served with me on the same squadron at about the same time. He and I had become quite close friends and living within a few miles of each other had kept in touch from time to time after demobilization. Our contact had diminished when I moved to Lincolnshire although we still exchanged Christmas cards.

His reason for calling unexpectedly was that he was camping at Mablethorpe with the Church Lads Brigade of which he was an officer. Finding himself with a free afternoon he had decided to look me up. I had no knowledge that he was in the vicinity nor of his membership of the CLB although I had known that he had been helping their band some years previously.

The curious feature is that he was wearing the summer uniform of CLB officers which was very similar to that affected as a working costume by Boor. He was also a very similar physical type.

It would seem that some definite image had been transmitted to my mind. However, the 'picture' had been confused by the unexpected dress my friend was wearing. At the time I was thinking of someone wearing similar clothing, of similar build and identified with the same period in my life, he must have been approaching the village on the bus.

The interesting thing to me is that the incident may disclose something of the way the mind sorts out an incoming impression and fits it to a known fact in the memory. Presumably what happened was that the mental process sorted the incoming image as best it could. That the image should be that of the man as he was at that moment rather than the personality I knew strikes me as odd.

This is not a dramatic case but it is one of great interest as it illustrates how an impression emerges from the subconscious and is 'sorted out' by the conscious mind and interpreted, often wrongly. What happened here, I feel, was that quite 'out of the blue' Mr Taylor had an impression of a bulky individual with heavy features dressed in a certain way. His conscious mind took over and asked, in effect, 'whom do I know who looks like that and is dressed like that?' and came up with the answer: 'Boor.' This was a wrong answer because it was Grant who tapped on the car window a few minutes later. This, therefore, is an example of precognition, as it concerns an impression of a man of a certain build and dressed in a certain way received a few minutes before a man answering to this description actually arrived and was recognized by Mr Taylor as an old friend.

In the late forties Mrs Lilian Dodd [pseudonym] was living in Bradford when she had a most vivid dream of seeing a group of people, including an old German lady and a year-old baby, neither of whom she had ever seen, sitting in 'a most unusual room' in her mother's large terrace house in Greenbank, Northwich, Cheshire.

Next day I travelled sixty miles to this same house to pay my mother a visit. I started back with a terrific shock as on opening the door the same group of people were sitting in exactly the same positions as in the dream. My mother had not told me that these people (most rare visitors, not old friends) had come to stay as she had been afraid I would not come if almost complete strangers were there. The old German lady on a visit from Hamburg and the baby were just as they were in the dream. Perhaps, as my mother and I were very close, and she was a very sensitive person, this was telepathy.

I wrote to Mrs Dodd about her experience. Her mother, she replied, took in one or two paying guests, and one of these, a schoolteacher, had married a German girl, whose mother remained in Hamburg. About six months before the dream the teacher, who then had a post in a Liverpool grammar school, had written to Mrs Dodd's mother to say that he would bring the baby he and his wife then had to see her sometime that summer and also that his wife's mother was paying them a visit sometime that year. Mrs Dodd had never seen the grandmother or the baby before, but she recognized them, and the position they were in, from her dream the night before. The 'most unusual room' was her mother's own private sitting-room which, until then, was kept exclusively for the use of the family. Boarders had the use of another room.

Mrs Dodd said that she had been told by her mother about the visit of the teacher and his wife and the baby, and the wife's mother, about six months before, but no date for the visit was given, and she had forgotten what she had been told.

My view of this case is that even if it is argued that Mrs Dodd knew in advance of this visit, and that therefore her dream was not truly precognitive, this does not explain away the fact that she 'saw' in her dream people she had never met before and that they were sitting in exactly the same position as they were in the dream in a room to which normally only the family had access.

'The dream and the actual happening were so alike that I really could not tell any difference,' said Mrs Dodd, who now lives in Ilkley, Yorkshire.

Mrs Angela Becker, of Claygate, Surrey, wrote to me after reading *Frontiers of the Unknown* saying, 'Here is an experience I had during the war. It is neither documented nor, probably for you, particularly unusual, but it has convinced me that precognition exists.'

At the time Mrs Becker was an officer in the Women's Auxiliary Air Force responsible for running a Bomber Command Senior WAAF non-commissioned officers' course at Husbands Bosworth, Leicestershire. Her story is an unusual one and is worth giving in some detail.

Each fortnight twenty-four WAAF NCOs were sent to me and during the fortnight I was responsible for giving them a refresher course in their duties as NCOs. I had a WAAF Flight/Sgt as my assistant. I lectured in a Nissen hut. At 10.15 each morning there was a break for coffee and at this time I came down from the rostrum and Flt/Sgt and I had our coffee with the NCOs, chatting about all sorts of things quite informally. In this way I got to know the NCOs. It was all a pretty friendly set up, anyway. One morning a rather ordinary girl approached me and said a little shyly 'I expect you are looking forward to this afternoon, aren't you, Ma'am?' I was a little surprised and answered that I hadn't really thought about it – it was going to be a pretty ordinary sort of afternoon: lecture on The Air Force Act as applied to the WAAF from 2-3, then drill, etc, etc. Quite pleasant, I thought, but nothing in it particularly to look forward to. It was then the NCO's turn to look surprised. 'Oh, I don't mean all *that,*' she said. 'I meant about your husband coming to see you.'

I answered 'But, my dear, my husband isn't coming to see me this afternoon.' 'Oh yes, Ma'am, he is,' she replied. 'I know he is.' 'But,' I said, 'you don't even know where he is stationed, do you?' 'No,' she replied, 'I don't even know whether he's in this country or not, but I do know he'll be here this afternoon. Of course, Ma'am, I thought you knew all about it, or I wouldn't have said anything!'

She seemed rather embarrassed. Then it was time to go back to work, but on the way I told my Flt/Sgt about what had been said and added that when my husband didn't put in an appearance I didn't want the matter referred to again for fear of upsetting the girl. I did just wonder why she had said this extraordinary thing and determined to keep an eye on her.

That afternoon, while I was giving the lecture, there came a tap on the door of the hut. My Flt/Sgt got up quickly to see who it was. I went on with my talk, then became aware of a rather startled looking Flt/Sgt waiting to talk to me. 'Your husband is outside, Ma'am,' was what she said! I went out to him and, to his surprise, said, 'Darling, you *must* tell me . . . when did you know you were coming down here?' He answered, 'Oh, round 10.30 this morning,' and went on to explain that his commanding officer called him in and said, 'Old boy, haven't you got a wife or popsie or something down at Husbands Bosworth? There's an Oxford to be ferried down – you'd better take it and spend the night and get back tomorrow.' So here I am – why?' Then I told him what had happened.

The next morning I said to the NCO who had predicted this, 'Well, you were right, weren't you? Does this often happen to you?' She answered naïvely, 'Oh, I knew you didn't believe me, Ma'am, but I just knew it was going to happen. I know these things, sometimes. It's never anything very important, but it's always happening to me. I'm used to it.' So that was that. I give you the account, for what it's worth. You are free to believe or disbelieve it. I tell it to you exactly as it happened.

I wrote to Mrs Becker, as she now is (she divorced the husband referred to in this case shortly after the war), and she said that the incident took place possibly in late 1944. She was unable to remember the name of the Flight Sergeant concerned.

It would be interesting if one could interview the NCO who had the precognitive experience as she seems to be gifted. Possibly she will read this account and get in touch with me. It seems that she 'picked up' telepathically the substance of the conversation relating to her officer that was taking place at another RAF station and knew that it concerned a visit from her husband that afternoon. Precognitive telepathy seems to be involved in this case.

There is no supporting evidence here. It is not a particularly important case, and certainly not dramatic, but it has the ring of truth about it.

I have not had many accounts of precognitive dreams or other experiences relating to a national event. One which is of interest came from Miss Eliot Bliss, whose experience in connection with the Trident crash is given in chapter four. In 1968, two weeks before the invasion of Czechoslovakia by Russia, she had a dream in which she was trying to hide along with another woman, a stranger, in a city quite unknown to her which was being invaded by a hostile power with a large number of tanks. Someone took them into a house and hid them. After a time they knew it was safe to go out. They crossed large thoroughfares with tall, oldish buildings on either side and foreign cars of a make she did not know. There were still tanks and armoured cars about, but she knew they were now out of danger.

When Miss Bliss woke up she had a feeling that this was a precognitive dream and told both her cousin and a friend living with her about it. When the Russian invasion took place she recognized from the scenes shown on TV the city she had seen in her dream and the houses. The cars were of Czech make, she now realized.

When I interviewed Miss Bliss, a lady who was with her confirmed that she had been told about this dream *before* the invasion of Czechoslovakia.

10 The British Premonitions Bureau

At 6 a.m. on 21 March 1967, the telephone rang in the home of Dr J. C. Barker, a consultant psychiatrist who had played a leading part in the setting-up of the British Premonitions Bureau earlier that year. His caller was Mr Alan Hencher, who was a night telephone operator for the Post Office, but was making this particular call from his home in Dagenham, Essex. Dr Barker listened with attention and made notes because he knew from experience that Mr Hencher had a precognitive gift, particularly for aircraft accidents.

In troubled tones Mr Hencher said, 'Aircraft Caravelle over mountains. Will be leaving in early morning between Monday and Sunday – it is going over mountains. It is going to radio that it is in trouble. Then it will cut out and there will be nothing. There are 123 or possibly 124 people on board. It is going to crash shortly after take-off. I can't tell exactly where or when it is going to happen. One person is saved in a very poor condition. I have had this feeling for a week, but it has been very strong in the past two-three days. . . .'

Dr Barker, in his notes on this case, points out that early on Thursday 20 April, a Britannia airliner crashed into a hilltop near Nicosia in Cyprus. In the London *Evening News* of 20 April, it stated that 124 persons had died and that rescuers had found 123 bodies.

For a later account of this disaster I turned to the report of the correspondent of *The Times* in Nicosia in the issue of 21 April. He said that only four people were saved from the 120 passengers and 10 crew of a Britannia owned by the Swiss Globe Air Company which had crashed early the previous day during a violent thunderstorm three miles from Nicosia airport.

The airliner was carrying tourists on a return flight from Bangkok and Bombay, bound for Cairo. Cairo airport, however, was closed owing to bad weather and the Britannia was diverted to Cyprus. Because of bad visibility the pilot, Captain Michael Muller, was unable at first to make a landing. He had made two attempts and was on a third run when radio contact was lost.

'The airliner appears to have hit a small hillock near the village of Lakatamia, then crashed into another hill and burst into flames.'

First reports that the airliner was struck by lightning were not favoured by officials, *The Times* correspondent said.

The survivors were treated in the Austrian-manned United Nations field hospital near Nicosia. Two were German and two Swiss. Three were seriously injured but one was almost unhurt.

At the time of this prediction Mr Hencher was forty-four and, according to Mrs Jennifer Preston who runs the British Premonitions Bureau from her home at Blackheath, South-East London, he 'loathed flying.' He has not been in touch with the Bureau for five years, and his present address is unknown. Before we go into the work of the Bureau it is worthwhile to analyse this particular case and to study Mr Hencher's gifts.

First, about Mr Hencher. After some successes in amateurish card guessing, he began to notice an ability to predict future events in 1953, two years after receiving a head wound in a car accident (this brings to mind Mr Peter Hurkos, the Dutch clairvoyant whose gift for psychometry developed after he fell thirty-six feet from a ladder in 1941, landing on his head and shoulder, which resulted in his being unconscious in hospital for three days). Mr Hencher told Mr Peter Fairley, then science correspondent of the London *Evening Standard* and co-founder with Dr Barker of the Bureau, that since the accident he 'gets regularly a sharp pain – like migraine – in my forehead which lasts half a minute, followed by a dull feeling of pain at the back of my head where I had my accident. Reporting the premonition gets rid of the headache.'

Premonitions, he found, took anything from five minutes to two weeks to develop. 'Sometimes I see things in black and white – sometimes in colour. I never get pleasure in premonitions. Often I get a figure in my mind, as though someone had spoken it. The details seem to come almost as headlines, and they come afterwards. As regards geographical location, I don't get place-names. I only see the immediate area and certain features. Occasionally I see words written, or see peoples' lips moving, but I'm not near enough to get a clear picture.'

Now for the hits and misses in Mr Hencher's prediction about the air disaster. He was wrong about the make of the plane, about the crash taking place shortly after take off, and about only one person being saved in a very poor condition. The number of people on board was 130.

But he had some impressive hits. The number of people killed was 126, which is very close to the 123 or 124 given in advance by Mr Hencher, and here we must remember that the London *Evening News* announced on the day of the accident, according to Dr Barker, that 124 persons had died and that rescuers had found 123 bodies (I will explain the significance of this a little later). The plane had passed over mountainous country before crashing into a hillside. Radio contact was lost before the crash.

It is significant, in my opinion, that for Mr Hencher 'the details seem to come almost as headlines', because there have been other cases in which the precognition takes the form of what is to be announced later by newspapers and *not* the true, or final, figure of casualties in a disaster.

In *Frontiers of the Unknown* (p. 108) I mention that in the well-known *La Plata* case, relating to the sinking of the SS *La Plata* during a storm in the Bay of Biscay on 29 November 1874, the first published account appeared in the *Daily Telegraph* of 3 December under the headline 'Terrible disaster at Sea. Loss of Sixty Lives', and that account was carried into the two main evening papers, the *Globe* and the *Pall Mall Gazette* on that date. A woman reported to her husband a dream she had had in which a ship turned upside down and sixty people were drowned. In the evening her husband returned home, threw an evening newspaper on the table, and said, 'Read your dream!' The last line of the report was 'and sixty people were drowned.' Assuming the observation 'sixty people were drowned' was a part of the woman's dream, it shows knowledge not of the correct figure, which was fifty-eight, but of the newspaper announcement, which gave sixty as the number lost, the survival of two men on a raft not having been reported. The fact that the dream occurred during the night before the announcement in the *Globe* fixes the night of the dream as that of 2/3 December.

If we assume that something of the same sort happened to Mr Hencher the experience he reported to Dr Barker applied to the first newspaper accounts of the air crash in Cyprus a month later.

On 1 May 1967 Mr Hencher had a premonition of a plane crash with many survivors and much sadness (Dr Barker asked him why and he replied 'children'). On 4 June an Argonaut belonging to British Midland Airways and *en route* from Palma, Majorca, to Manchester, crashed at Stockport. Of the seventy-nine men, women and children on board sixty-nine died as the result of the impact or fire, and of the crew of five three were killed. Thus there were twelve survivors. Among the dead there were a number of children.

In a letter to Mr Hencher, Dr Barker asked, 'You laid much stress on the tail fin. Why?'

The reason for his question was that in all the news pictures of the crash and on TV, the tail fin was featured prominently as it was the only part of the plane that was more or less intact.

It seems that here, as in the Cyprus plane crash, Mr Hencher 'picked up' something in the form of how it would be featured in later newspapers or TV programmes.

Dreams, it seems, did not play much part in Mr Hencher's precognitive experiences. It was interesting, and a little sad, to see Dr Barker's comments on Mr Hencher's prediction of his early death in correspondence dated 1967 when I examined some of the records of the Bureau at Mrs Preston's home (I had two interviews with her). Dr Barker died the following year at the early age of forty-four.

When Dr Barker was consultant psychiatrist at Shelton Hospital, Shrewsbury, he visited Aberfan on the day following the disaster in which 144 persons were killed, 'and was appalled by the devastation and suffering I saw everywhere,' he said in an article in the *Journal* of the SPR for December 1967. 'It then occurred to me that there might have been people, not necessarily in the Aberfan area, but possibly throughout Britain, who had experienced some forewarning of this disaster, possibly in the form of a strong premonition. Since the Aberfan disaster was such an unusual one, I considered that it would provide an excellent opportunity to investigate precognition.'

Dr Barker therefore telephoned Mr Fairley, who launched an appeal in the *Evening Standard* requesting persons claiming any foreknowledge of the Aberfan disaster to communicate with him, describing their experiences. Mr Fairley's appeal was widely syndicated. Within two weeks Dr Barker had received a total of seventy-six replies from persons living in various parts of England. Almost immediately after Mr Fairley's appeal had appeared, the Psychophysical Research Unit at Oxford issued a press release asking for cases of precognition of the Aberfan disaster and a national newspaper launched a further appeal. It was estimated that altogether nearly 200 persons claimed to have had some foreknowledge of the Aberfan disaster.

Of the seventy-six letters Dr Barker received, sixty required further investigation. He wrote to all the correspondents requesting the names and addresses of witnesses who could confirm, if possible, that the writer's experiences had been related to them before the Aberfan disaster occurred, and received the required confirmation in twenty-four cases.

Thirty-six letters were from dreamers. The remainder claimed to have had visions of the disaster or parts of it, or else developed a sense of intense unease for a variable interval before the tragedy occurred. In a few instances an impending disaster was sensed clairvoyantly at spiritual 'home-circle' gatherings.

Dr Barker lists thirty-five ostensible precognitive experiences in his study of the disaster in the SPR *Journal*.

As a result of his investigation Dr Barker considered that the public should be invited to report their premonitions to a central bureau, perhaps linked with a computer, to detect 'peaks' or patterns in the incoming material and to help exclude false, trivial or irrelevant information. 'Such a project would require to be well advertised in the first instance with periodic reminders through the national press, radio and television programmes. An official "early warning" could then be issued only if the place, date or nature of an impending disaster became clear.'

The British Premonitions Bureau began operations in January 1967. In its first year it received about 500 premonitions of natural disasters, disasters involving planes and other vehicles, political events, deaths and assassinations. Most predictions in 1967 were of air crashes, with earthquakes second.

In February 1969, the Bureau came under the control of the *TV Times*, a weekly magazine which also publishes features of general interest and programmes of commercial radio stations. Mr Fairley is science editor of this publication.

The Bureau records the premonitions it receives in the following categories: air and space; road, rail, sea; royal family; personalities; politics, war, riots; economy; crime; sport; natural disasters; explosions, fire, collapse of buildings; miscellaneous.

The Bureau does not record premonitions if they are of a purely personal nature, such as that of the impending death of a member of the family. This is understandable. Mrs Preston has to run the Bureau virtually single-handed and inquiries into cases of a personal nature can take up a great deal of time, as I know from experience.

Since the British Premonitions Bureau was set up, over 3,000 reports of alleged precognition have been received but not all have been recorded.

Cases recorded are filed under the following categories: dreams; audio-visual; impressions; and 'others', which include messages received through mediums, automatic writing, etc.

The proportions of the 1,206 recorded cases received up to 31 October 1973, are as follows: dreams, ten per cent; audio-visual, seventy per cent; impressions, five per cent; others, fifteen per cent.

I was greatly surprised to notice the low proportion of precognitive dreams and will comment on the significance of this in the final chapter.

When Dr Barker went through the case reports relating to Aberfan he found that seven people (four men and three women) developed non-specific symptoms of acute mental and physical unease from four days to a few hours before the Aberfan disaster. He asked:

> Is this perhaps a hitherto unrecognized medical or psychosomatic syndrome akin to the phenomenon known as the 'sympathetic projection of pain?' Could the symptoms reported by these persons depend upon some sort of telepathic 'shock wave' induced by a disaster? Speculations are rife, but clearly these so-called 'human disaster reactors' appear to require much further study, including perhaps full medical and psychiatric investigation. In the meantime I have requested all seven of them to communicate with me *immediately* whenever they experience

their familiar symptoms in order to ascertain whether they are significant or merely false alarms. In view of the frequency of disasters occurring throughout the world this may prove to be a formidable undertaking.

Mrs Preston said that the bulk of the premonitions recorded came from six people. I have already mentioned Mr Hencher. Another is a woman journalist in the provinces who wishes to remain anonymous. She was unwilling to give me any information, mainly because she was writing a book about her own experiences, but there are some records of these in the Bureau.

On 21 November 1968, this lady had a premonition of young children being trapped and mass death. She could not see fire or understand the reason for panic, and the children all seemed to rush to one end of the room and suffer there.

On 25 November fourteen children died in a blaze in a home for mentally retarded children at Beauvais, France.

She had a premonition on 22 January 1970, of Mr Harold Wilson, then Prime Minister, stumbling down stairs which seemed to have metal on them. Six days later Mr Wilson was badly bruised in a fall at the British Embassy in Washington. He slipped on a highly polished marble floor and fell against a door, cutting his lip on the metal door handle, hurting ribs and wrist (the stairs at the Embassy do not seem to have been the cause of this accident, but the reference to metal is significant).

On 29 January the same year, this lady had a premonition of two quite young children who seemed to be together in some kind of trouble, perhaps disaster. One seemed to have curly hair and was about two years old. On 6 April, curly-haired three-year-old twins died when they were trapped in a disused refrigerator.

On 5 June 1970, she reported that TV would be interrupted by a news flash. On 29 June, TV programmes were interrupted by the news of the death of the first wife of Mr Jeremy Thorpe, the Liberal Party leader, in a road accident.

The same day this lady reported a drama, probably a tragedy, perhaps involving only one person, in connection with the World Cup. That month a football fan was knocked down in Mexico and died in a coma eight weeks later. His parents faced a £4,000 bill.

Another member of the 'team' of six is Lorna Middleton, a

medium and teacher of dancing, who has a gift for predicting national disasters. But not all her predictions are on this scale.

For instance, on 30 December 1967, she predicted a bad crash, involving a lorry with an exceptionally heavy load. Seven days later twelve people were killed when an express train hit a low loader carrying a giant transformer at Hixon level-crossing.

One of the Bureau's correspondents gave a detailed description on 26 March 1969, of a woman being washed up on the beach of a rocky coast where a car was waiting for her.

On 7 April a woman was washed ashore near Cherbourg, where the coast is rocky. She was guided to the beach by the headlights of a car.

Some interesting predictions came from unexpected places. One on 31 January 1969, from Broadmoor (a special hospital run by the Department of Health and Social Security for people who require treatment under conditions of special security on account of their dangerous, violent or criminal propensities), predicted the collapse of a radio/TV mast for no apparent reason.

On 19 March that year, a 1,200 foot television mast fell under the weight of tons of ice at Emley Moor, near Huddersfield.

Five newspapers are delivered to Mrs Preston's home every day. She reads these thoroughly to see if any of the news items apply to premonitions sent in by her correspondents. Beyond this it is not possible for her to do any 'follow up' research.

Early in 1968, Dr Barker visited America and spoke at a meeting of the American Society for Psychical Research about the formation of the British Premonitions Bureau. As a result, the Central Premonitions Registry was started in New York City in June, 1968.

Has the British Premonitions Bureau achieved the objects for which it was set up?

A great deal of interesting material has come to light but so far there has not been the same number of premonitions applied to any single case such as those which preceded the sinking of the *Titanic*, the Aberfan disaster, or, to a lesser extent, the crash of the airship R101. Possibly this is because they were, in their own way, unique and the subject of a great deal of emotion. However, I feel that the Bureau has been successful in bringing to light a number of people who seem to have a gift for precognition. It would be most rewarding if they could be interviewed in depth to see if they have other paranormal gifts, such as for telepathy and clairvoyance, and to discover if their precognitive experiences also include occasional ones of retrocognition (the 'seeing' of events in the past). All experimenters are short of gifted subjects. For this reason it might be advisable for the SPR to seek closer links with the Bureau.

11 Some conclusions

We have now reached that stage when the reader may look back on a large number of cases and draw his own conclusions from them, just as a jury may look back on the evidence which has just been presented in a court case and draw conclusions from the testimony of the witnesses. A great deal will depend on the value the reader places on human testimony. I suggest that much of the evidence is strong, particularly in the cases in chapters one and two, where the experiences were committed to writing before the fulfilment of the event recorded. The evidence in Mrs Hellström's case of the Coptic rose is particularly strong. It may be argued, of course, that this was not a dramatic case and did not involve anything particularly important. I disagree, because in my view it is the evidential value of a case that counts, be it important or not. As H. F. Saltmarsh points out in the chapter on evidence and classification in *Foreknowledge*, 'trivial details are evidentially more valuable than broad general features.' An example of this is given in my book in chapter nine in which Mrs Aspinall told her husband about seeing shattered glass all over the road (he confirmed this) not long before they were involved in a road accident in which glass *was* scattered all over the road. Other examples could be given.

If we accept, on the basis of the evidence presented here, that experiences involving precognition do occur it follows logically that we must abandon the concept of one-dimensional time or, as I prefer to call it, linear time, i.e. time as represented by a straight line, with the past behind us, the present as the moment in which the eye and brain take in what is written here, and the future as all that stretches before us. When a person has a precognitive experience he is not plunged, if that is the word, into the as yet undisclosed future; he is having the experience here and now, which is the present. Thus the future, which may be some moments or years away, is joined to the present while the experience is taking place. I have put this in the simplest possible way so that the concept may be grasped.

But when we reason why this should be so we are immediately in difficulties. 'How can the experience be a response to events which have not yet come about?' the bewildered reader asks. Half a dozen other objections come to mind, including those of predestination or free will.

We are thus in the position of accepting, as I do on the evidence, that precognitive experiences take place but being unable to explain how. One possible answer has been suggested by Mr H. A. C. Dobbs with his theory of two dimensional time. In quantum physics I feel we have a framework in which some of the answers to the paradox of precognition may be found. I also feel that we should concentrate on the insights of some of the more advanced physicists rather than argue endlessly about the theories I have outlined in my introduction. Dunne, for all his virtues, has not had the last word.

One of the best books I know for background reading on the scientific and psychological approach to ESP is *Psychology and Psychical Research* by the late Professor Sir Cyril Burt, published a few years ago by the SPR. In the section headed 'Behind the World of Physics', he points out that the most outspoken present-day critics of parapsychology – Professor C. E. M. Hansel, Dr J. G. Taylor, and their various followers – still take their stand on the old materialist assumptions which form the basis of 'classical' physics. The universe is regarded as essentially a purely physical world, and by this they mean a completely mechanical world. They still cling to the traditional notion of absolute space as a kind of pre-existent void; and with it they retain the Newtonian concept of an independent one-dimensional time. All events are held to take place within this empty framework, and to be causally determined by preceding events in accordance with the strictest laws of mechanics. Sir Cyril writes:

Obviously such a conception, as Professor Hansel rightly argues, would be quite incompatible with the anomalous phenomena reported by parapsychologists. Indeed, strictly interpreted, it would seem to rule out the possibility, not only of mind, but of life. I suggest, however, that what Broad has called the 'basic limiting principles' of science – which, as he says, are all negative – should be constructed as dictating, not what is impossible, but merely what is highly improbable. . . . Were it not for the mechanistic preconceptions which these 'limiting principles' imply, most impartial readers would assuredly accept the ostensible evidence in favour of paranormal phenomena as providing at least a strong *prima facie* case; and, I think, there is almost equally good evidence to show that these phenomena are in fact inexplicable in terms of any known physical hypothesis.

Sir Cyril goes on to say that Professor Hansel cites no living physicist who now accedes to these 'limiting principles' or endorses the scepticism based upon them. 'Indeed, of the few leading physicists today who have expressed any views on the matter nearly all have declared their sympathy with the aims of psychical research.' He continues:

However, Professor Hansel's criticisms gain a superficial plausibility from the fact that most writers on parapsychology tend to adopt much the same traditional scheme. This is evident in many current books and papers dealing with such phenomena as precognition, retrocognition, and 'out-of-the-body experiences'. Indeed these very expressions show how completely, though no doubt unconsciously, the writers remain addicted to this mode of thinking. It leads inevitably to difficulties and paradoxes for the parapsychologist, which on a closer scrutiny turn out to be no more than pseudo-problems, arising from these obsolete postulates and designations.

What then, the psychologist naturally asks, are the reasons for these fallacious assumptions? Partly, I fancy, its seductive appeal for those who want simple answers to complex questions.

There are no simple answers to complex questions in psychical research, particularly that aspect of ESP known as precognition. It will be seen that I am in good company when I suggest that we should move away from 'classical' physics when we try to find the answers to some of the problems we have been considering here.

Sir Cyril quotes the views of Professor Broad. These are amplified in his introduction to my book *Frontiers of the Unknown* and are well worth quoting at this stage because they support what Sir Cyril has been saying:

In considering, and attaching very great weight to, those fundamental principles as to the general constitution and ways of working of the physical world which are taken as the framework of contemporary science, we should bear the following fact in mind. The Theory of Relativity and the Uncertainty Principle have introduced the most radical changes. These involve, unlike earlier scientific developments, not just the addition or the modification of laws falling within the hitherto accepted general scheme. They involve extremely fundamental modifications *in that scheme itself*. Some of these are as paradoxical to the everyday scientist, who is not an expert in quantum mechanics, as they are to ordinary common sense. Now, what is offered as the scientifically accepted scheme of the constitution and ways of working of nature is almost invariably that which *was* accepted before the making of these radical changes, which are so fundamental and so paradoxical that only a few contemporary scientists are generally aware of them and only a very small minority of experts are at home with them. It might well be that phenomena, which could not be fitted into the older accepted scientific scheme of nature, could be housed without much difficulty within the profoundly modified scheme which is now emerging from the labours of the quantum physicists.

Note the use of the word 'emerging'. There is no suggestion here that science has had the last word. But then, of course, science, when correctly understood, never claims to have had the last word. Many people, faced by phenomena which they do not understand, cling to 'science' as a support for their ideas of time, space and causality (ideas now outmoded, as we have seen) for the same reason that a drunken man, uncertain of his direction and the way the signposts are pointing, clings to a lamppost. It, at least, is something solid and familiar.

But perhaps this remark is a little unfair. Mr Arthur Koestler, in his section of *The Challenge of Chance* (Random House, 1973) which he has written with Sir Alister Hardy and Mr Robert Harvie, states that 'quantum physics is an esoteric discipline beyond the grasp of the educated layman.'

Consider the implications of the following passage by Mr Koestler:

In those first, magical decades of the century, Einstein, de Broglie and Schrödinger between them dematerialized matter like the conjuror who makes the lady vanish from the curtained box on the stage. Heisenberg replaced determinism by the principle of indeterminancy and causality by probability. Dirac postulated holes in space stuffed with electrons of *negative mass*. Thomson made a single particle go through two holes in a screen at the same time – which, Sir Cyril Burt commented, is more than a ghost can do. Protons – packets of light – devoid of mass were observed in the process of giving virgin birth to twin particles endowed with solid mass; Feynman made time flow backward on his diagrams. To paraphrase an old saying: inside the atom is where things happen that don't. Yet these were not crank theories: each of the physicists whom I mentioned received a Nobel prize for his contribution to the surrealistic panorama which modern physics has substituted for the tangible world.

Holes in space . . . time flowing backwards. These are concepts so unfamiliar that the mind at first refuses to accept them, just as it often refuses to accept the concept of precognition.

This is a fitting moment to introduce the question of coincidence, which is the great 'let out' for critics who wish to explain away any single seemingly paranormal event as 'merely a coincidence'. Let us take once again Mrs Aspinall's case. She had a vision of shattered glass on the road and, the critic would argue, it was just a coincidence that shortly afterwards the car in which she was riding was involved in an accident and shattered glass was scattered on the road. Every responsible writer on psychical research makes allowance for the fact that coincidences do occur. I have no doubt that some of the cases in this book can be ascribed to coincidence. But can they all be ascribed to this cause? I would say that it is impossible. If the critic objects that 'nothing is impossible in the type of case you have been discussing' let us consider just one case, that of the man who had the feeling of physical cold and of fear which he confessed to his wife shortly before he was killed in a road crash. If he often felt cold and frightened the symptoms of cold and the confession of fear would be understandable and coincidence could, perhaps, be ascribed to the accident that followed on this particular occasion, but, as his wife makes clear in her account, her husband, 'a most prosaic person, very down to earth and not given to imagining things,' was not a man who showed symptoms of physical cold for no apparent reason or expressed himself as being afraid. On the one occasion that he did he was killed shortly afterwards.

However, if the critic still clings to 'coincidence' as the probable explanation for most of the cases I have been discussing, with 'faulty reporting', 'unreliable memory', and so on as an explanation for the rest, it is worthwhile making a note of the fact that writers such as Mr Koestler are now questioning the assumption that the coincidences do not have meaningful significance. There are certainly coincidences which are trivial but there are also coincidences which are meaningful. Mr Koestler says in *The Challenge of Chance*:

> Whether one believes that some highly improbable coincidences are manifestations of some unknown principle operating beyond physical causality, or are produced by that immortal monkey at the typewriter, is ultimately a matter of inclination and temperament; the point I shall try to make is that *no amount of scientific knowledge can help a person to decide which of these alternative beliefs is more reasonable or nearer to the truth.* I have found to my surprise that the majority of my acquaintances – among whom scientists predominate – are inclined towards the first alternative, although some are reluctant to admit it, for fear of ridicule, even to themselves.

Mr Koestler discusses certain coincidental cases as part of a 'clustering' or 'converging' of events which are meaningfully related but causally unrelated. In some such cases telepathy seems to be involved and in others precognition. Take the following extraordinary case which concerns some of the crosswords in the London *Daily Telegraph* immediately preceding the allied invasion of Europe – D-Day, 6 June 1944. The codewords referring to various operations were perhaps the best kept secrets of the war, Mr Koestler says. The codename for the entire invasion plan was *Overlord*. For the naval operations: *Neptune*. The two Normandy beaches chosen for landing the American task force were referred to as *Utah* and *Omaha*. And the artificial harbours that were to be placed in position off the beaches were called *Mulberry*.

The first codeword appeared in the solution of crossword 5775 in the *Daily Telegraph* of 3 May: *Utah*. The second on 23 May: *Omaha*. The third on 31 May: *Mulberry*. The fourth and fifth – the principal codewords – appeared on 2 June, four days before D-Day: *Neptune* and *Overlord*.

'MI5 was called in to investigate. The crosswords had been composed by Mr Leonard Sidney Dawe, a schoolmaster who lived in Leatherhead, Surrey. He had been the *Daily Telegraph*'s senior crossword compiler for more than twenty years. He had not known that the words he used were codewords, and had not the foggiest idea how they had come into his head.'

It is stretching the meaning of the word 'coincidence' very far when we apply it to a case such as this one. Possibly the working of an unknown law is involved here, and if so, the use of the phrase 'it was just a coincidence' to explain away some strange cases in psychical research does not have the impact or validity it had.

Mr Koestler says that the invasion of codewords in the crosswords 'could conceivably be explained by a strong telepathic effect generated by a vital secret shared by thousands of anxious men.' But Mr Koestler presents this case, as I do, as an example of precognition, and this leads me logically to my next point.

As I completed the chapters in my book I made a summary of the types of experience involved, such as dreams, visual, auditory, or impressions, and soon found myself in difficulties. Some of Mrs Hellström's experiences were described by her as a dream and vision combined (chapter one). In chapter nine, the strange case from Australia, Mrs Marshall heard a loud voice which said 'Helen has hurt her leg' and then experienced a vision of the headmaster bringing her daughter home in his car which he did more than three hours later. Should this case be classed under the heading of 'visions' or 'auditory hallucinations' or both? Two types of experience were involved in the one case but if I put them in separate columns without explanation the reader could assume that the statistics contained two cases instead of one. In the case which heads chapter nine, Mrs Davis tells with supporting evidence how she 'knew' that ex-Ambassador Bullitt was dead some days before the actual date of death but she was uncertain how she gained the information, suggesting that it could have been by 'hearing' it on the radio, 'seeing' it on television, or 'reading' it in a newspaper. How is this case to be classified? Certainly not under the heading of 'impressions' because she did not have an impression that Bullitt, a man in whom she had no interest, was dead; she 'read', 'saw' or 'heard' it, but could not remember the form in which the information had come to her. In the same chapter I give the case of the NCO who told Mrs Becker, to her surprise, that her husband was going to visit her that afternoon, which he did. The girl presumably 'picked up' the information by telepathy at the same time as Mrs Becker's then husband was being told by his commanding officer that he could take a plane to the airfield where his wife was stationed. How should this case be classified? The girl did not gain the information by 'seeing' or 'hearing' anything and what she had was something much stronger and more specific than an impression: it related to a visit that was to be made by Mrs Becker's husband that afternoon and not at some indefinite time in the future. Perhaps the case should be classified as one of precognitive telepathy.

This leads me to the conclusion that precognition cannot be considered as an isolated phenomenon but as a manifestation of one aspect of ESP. This has been pointed out before by researchers such as Dr Thouless and Dr D. J. West, but it is worth saying again for the benefit of new readers. Dr Thouless says in *From Anecdote to Experiment in Psychical Research* that his colleague Dr B. P. Wiesner and he 'were inclined to think that there might be no real difference between what were called telepathy, clairvoyance, and precognition, that they might be the same capacity working under different circumstances'. Dr West says in *Psychical Research Today* (p. 93): 'Telepathy, clairvoyance, precognition, precognitive telepathy – they are entirely hypothetical interpretations of how ESP works. It is simpler to forget them, and look upon ESP as a single entity, which has been demonstrated under various experimental conditions.'

It was necessary for me to point out the difficulties in classifying certain cases because now we must consider the classification of the cases given in this book. It is not possible to classify all cases under the same heading for various reasons, i.e. certain cases defy classification, some cases I have quoted from the literature of psychical research, such as in accounts of the cross-correspondences, have come to us with little information of the form the 'message' took, and as the British Premonitions Bureau puts a certain type of case in a table under the general heading of audio-visual it is not possible to compare such cases with others listed under two separate headings.

So let us take the statistics of the British Premonitions Bureau given here for the first time, although I must allow for the possibility that they may appear in a magazine before this book is published.

It is most surprising that 70 per cent of the 1,206 recorded cases should come under the heading of audio-visual and that only 10 per cent should be dreams.

The low percentage of dream cases in the Bureau's total is contrary to all the findings recorded to date.

Professor Stevenson sets out the position in his paper 'Precognition of Disasters' in the *Journal* of the SPR for April 1970, from which I have already quoted.

> It was early noted in the SPR studies of precognition that these experiences tended to occur more often when the subject was asleep and dreaming than when he was awake. Thus in the 1888 series (recorded in a paper by Mrs E. M. Sidgwick 'On the evidence for premonitions') 66 per cent of the experiences occurred during dreaming, in the 1934 series (a report by Mr H. F. Saltmarsh) 68.1 per cent were reported to occur during dreaming, and in the 1957 series (an analysis of spontaneous cases by Miss Celia Green), 68.8 per cent were reported as occurring during dreaming. Very similar figures were found in the American series in which 68 per cent occurred during dreaming (a report by Dr Louisa E. Rhine in 1954) and in the German series in which 60 per cent occurred during dreaming (a report by G. Sannwald in 1959).

Why should there be this difference between the Bureau's findings and those hitherto recorded?

There are two possible reasons for this. The first, and possibly the most important, is that premonitions of a personal nature are not sent to the Bureau. As Dr Louisa E. Rhine points out in *ESP in Life and Lab* 'Precognitive experiences are probably nearly as common as acorns under oak trees. But what are they concerned with? Bits and snatches from an individual's daily life?' If 'bits and snatches from an individual's daily life' are excluded from a collection of ostensible precognitive experiences the result is bound to be distorted (when I make this comment I do have in mind the purpose for which the Bureau was set up, which was not to record personal experiences of a minor nature). The second possible reason is that the bulk of the experiences recorded at the Bureau come from six individuals who are probably strong visualizers (auditory experiences account for only a small proportion of cases involving ostensible ESP, I have found in the course of my research).

For instance, among the sixty or so precognitive experiences recorded in Mrs Hellström's case books only six were of an auditory nature and forty-two were visions in colour. Only thirteen experiences came in dream form.

The results of the survey by the British Premonitions Bureau, taken in conjunction with the analysis of Mrs Hellström's experiences, are clearly important because they provide an answer to the critics who assert that because millions of people dream every night, and one person might have several dreams, it is obvious that some of these dreams are bound to come true. It is part of the same argument that people will report the few dreams that are fulfilled and ignore the great bulk of their dreams which are unfulfilled. If it can be shown, as it has by the Bureau's findings and by the analysis of Mrs Hellström's cases, that a small number of gifted people have most of their precognitive experiences *when awake* the evidence for precognition in spontaneous cases is immeasurably strengthened.

It must be remembered in this connection that dreams are hallucinations, as are experiences when awake (for an interpretation of hallucination I refer the reader back to the closing portions of my introduction), but while one person may have several dreams during the course of a night, no one I have ever met or heard about in the course of my researches has had several experiences involving ESP *when awake* in the course of a day or in succeeding days.

Now for the experiences related by my own correspondents. I have selected accounts sent in by twenty-six people or given in newspapers and followed up by me. Sometimes the correspondents gave accounts of a number of incidents, and the total number of experiences selected for this book has been confined to thirty-five. Selection was obviously necessary. It must be remembered, in assessing my figures, that many experiences of a trivial or personal nature or lacking verification have been excluded.

Thirteen experiences were impressions when awake, eleven were dreams, eight visions, one was an auditory hallucination, one a tactile hallucination and one (Mrs Davis's experience in chapter nine) could not be classified.

Eleven experiences were concerned with death, eight with plane crashes, six with danger to a person or a premonition of an accident, three were of a visionary nature concerned with something significant in the future, two were of a trivial or a personal nature, and one was a dream of an event of national importance (the invasion of Czechoslovakia). The reason for the difference between this total (thirty-one) and the number of experiences (thirty-five) is that in two cases more than one experience related to the same incident.

I have not included in the above figures the case in which the Baines's family dog, Merry, showed ostensible precognition of the bombing of the house at Wimbledon (chapter six). If this is an example of true precognition, as it seems to be, we have no means of knowing how the information was obtained by the dog. This case raises the total number of experiences related by my correspondents and published in this book to thirty-six. Cases recorded by Mrs Hellström and the British Premonitions Bureau are not, of course, included in this total.

Some consideration should be given to the significance of the time element – that is, the interval between the experience and the fulfilment of it – in precognitive experiences. In his report on the Aberfan disaster Dr Barker pointed out that Mr G. W. Lambert had, in a paper in the SPR *Journal* in 1965, enumerated five *desiderata*, all of which were necessary to establish any connection between a dream and a future event.

They were:

1. The dream should be reported to a credible witness before the occurrence of the event to which it appears to relate.

2. The time interval between the dream and the event should be short.

3. The event should be one in which the circumstances of the dreamer seemed improbable at the time of the dream.

4. The description in the dream should be of an event destined to be literally fulfilled and not merely symbolically foreshadowed.

5. The details of the dream should tally with the details of the event.

In the second of these conditions Mr Lambert seems to follow Dunne, both believing that the possibility that the dream and the event are linked by chance coincidence increases as the time interval increases. However, I have reservations about this as it excludes long term precognition as shown in the surgeon's and

Lady Namier's experiences (chapter eight) and some of Mrs Hellström's experiences (chapter one).

At this stage, if experience is anything to go by, the reader will probably be asking 'What are your own views on precognition? Have you got your own theory on it? Have you had a precognitive experience yourself?'

I think that many people experience precognition quite often in a very minor way. You think of someone whom you have not seen or heard from for many years and then you get a letter from him or meet him unexpectedly in the street. You ring for the fifth or sixth time a number which has been engaged every time you rang but this time you *know* that the number will be disengaged and it is. I have had a few seemingly precognitive experiences but they have not been important ones, I have no supporting evidence, and as I am not the best judge of my own experiences I will not give them. But personal experience is clearly important as it carries more conviction than anything else. In his book *The Politics of Experience* (Pantheon, 1967), Dr R. D. Laing, discussing social phenomenology, says: '*only* experience is evident. Experience is the *only* evidence.' It is possible for people to argue that individuals in good mental and physical health cannot see apparitions because 'there's no such thing as a ghost', but anyone who has studied the evidence with an open mind must accept that people do see apparitions, and the person who has himself experienced an apparition will reply: 'But this happened to me. You may say that it cannot happen. I cannot deny my own experience.'

The same argument, of course, applies to precognitive experiences.

Now for my own views on precognition. The cases which carry the most conviction for me are those with unusual details – the train with green carriages seen by Mrs Hellström, her case of the Coptic rose, Mrs Aspinall's experience of seeing shattered glass on the road before her own accident, Mr Taylor's experience of thinking about a man who dressed in a distinctive way but whom he had not seen for many years just before a man who was dressed in that way tapped on his car window. Another example concerns the colour of the mechanics' uniforms in Sir Victor Goddard's visionary experience of a wartime airfield.

A case which admirably illustrates this point is given in the biography of Mark Twain by Albert Bigelow Paine (Harper and Bros, New York, 1912). When Mark Twain was a young man of about twenty, he and his brother Henry worked on a Mississippi river boat running between St Louis and New Orleans. One night when Mark Twain was sleeping at his sister's house in St Louis, he had the following vivid dream: 'He saw Henry a corpse, lying in a metallic burial case in the sitting-room, supported on two chairs. On his breast lay a bouquet of flowers, with a single crimson bloom in the centre.'

When Mark Twain awoke in the morning the dream had been so vivid that he believed his brother had died and when he rose and dressed he thought he would go into his sister's sitting-room and look at his dead brother. But he changed his mind and went for a walk instead. He had walked to the middle of the block when he suddenly realized that he had only dreamed that his brother was dead. He returned to the house and told the dream to his sister.

A few weeks later, however, Mark Twain and his brother separated in New Orleans and returned towards St Louis in separate ships. Four boilers of the *Pennsylvania*, the ship Henry was on, blew up with an enormous loss of life. Henry was badly injured and after a few days of terrible suffering he died in Memphis, Tennessee. Although most of the victims of this disaster were buried in simple wooden coffins, some ladies of Memphis had become specially moved by the plight of the youthful Henry Clemens and they subscribed for a metal coffin for him. When Mark Twain went to see his brother's corpse laid out with the others, he found it in a metal coffin just as he had seen it in his dream, but without any bouquet of flowers. As he stood by the coffin a lady entered and placed on the breast of Henry's body a bouquet of white flowers with one red rose in the centre.

The single red bloom, foreseen in the dream, gives this case its distinctive character.

A case in which a single object is involved, such as the Coptic rose or a red bloom, is not ambiguous in terms of interpretation. There are cases which are more impressive in terms of content – Aberfan and the sinking of the *Titanic*, for instance – but difficulties of interpretation of visionary or dream experiences can arise. Take as an example Abraham Lincoln's dream which occurred a few days before his assassination, and described by him to several reliable witnesses the following morning. He dreamt that, feeling disturbed, he got up and went downstairs, heard people sobbing, but wandered from room to room without ever seeing anybody. Finally he arrived in the East Room of the White House, where in a bad light he could just see a body lying in state and soldiers doing guard duty round it. He asked one of the soldiers whose body was lying there and was told it was the President's. Mr J. B. Priestley, discussing this case in *Over the Long High Wall* (Heinemann, 1972), says that he cannot deny it an element of prevision, but goes on:

> As far as Lincoln was concerned, this was an anxiety dream on a grand imaginative scale. There was every excuse for his having such a dream. During the last phase of the Civil War, Lincoln, hated in the South and disliked by various factions in the North, was constantly receiving letters that were insanely abusive and threatening. He may have shrugged them away but that does not mean they would have no effect on his unconscious, which finally created for him the dream he described. This dream deserves its fame but not as an example of precognition.

I do not have my own theory on precognition, which is one of the subjects beyond our present understanding. I may, however, suggest one or two pointers to areas where a solution may be found. A new understanding of the world we live in is emerging, I feel, from the labours of the quantum physicists. Dr D. J. West points out in *Psychical Research Today* that the 'worst difficulty of all in the acceptance of precognition is the seemingly inescapable corollary that the effect can precede the cause,' but this is not a difficulty for the quantum physicist, who is also accustomed to such concepts as time flowing backwards. However, it is unlikely that an adequate theory about precognition will be evolved apart from one which takes account of other aspects of ESP, and there is as yet no adequate theory that can explain psychic phenomena and fit them into a scientific framework.

Another area which will repay study as a pointer to some aspects of precognition is that of consciousness. Sir Cyril Burt, in *Psychology and Psychical Research*, after discussing the work on the brain of such eminent neurophysiologists as Sherrington and Eccles, says that their researches suggest that the brain is designed to function not as a generator of consciousness, 'but as a detector, selector, amplifier, and two-way transmitter of consciousness.' Anyone who has studied, as I have, a great many spontaneous cases is drawn irresistibly to the conclusion, that what is involved in such cases is an interlinking of consciousness spanning both space and time.

It will have been noted in the introduction that Mr Dobbs talked about 'interaction between brains.' I cannot help wondering whether 'interaction between brains' is an adequate explanation for some types of precognition. Suppose, for instance, a man had a dream in which he had just driven in his car round a corner in the mountains to be faced with an avalanche of great boulders falling on the road immediately in front of him and one such boulder being on the point of falling on his car. No other brain is involved in this. The accident happens the following morning in exactly the same circumstances as were forecast in the dream, but fortunately the dreamer survives to tell his tale. However, the dream may have been 'picked up' telepathically by other dreamers. They could not affect the outcome of the dream, as they did not know the dreamer, but it is just possible that among them there was one who did know the dreamer, knew where he was staying at that particular time, and took the opportunity to telephone him and advise him to be careful. There are no simple solutions to problems such as this.

Mr Dobbs also speaks of 'common sense' rejecting the concept of direct acquaintance with a not yet existent future. I have reservations about this point of view. As Dr Thouless points out in *From Anecdote to Experiment in Psychical Research*:

The natural thing to do with stories of alleged paranormal phenomena is to pass them by with the assurance that they can't be true because they conflict with 'common sense'. It is not surprising that many people do reject the paranormal on this ground and that they are inclined to regard a research interest in it as somewhat eccentric. Yet there is at least strong enough evidence for some of the alleged paranormal phenomena to create a case for further inquiry, and there are good grounds for distrusting common sense as a guide to what is possible and what is not possible. 'Common sense' may be the name we give to nothing more authoritative than the thought habits that we happen to have derived from our ordinary experience. These thought habits certainly do not lead us to expect that our actions can be influenced by the thought of another person unless he expresses his thought in speech or in some other way. Nor do our thought habits lead us to expect that light will bend round corners. Our common sense proves to be an unreliable guide to what we have not experienced, whether this is the diffraction of light or the properties of sub-atomic particles; it cannot be allowed to have a decisive voice in determining our attitude towards the paranormal.

In a later section of his book (p. 140) Dr Thouless states that 'if the facts of precognition are in conflict with our customary ways of thinking about time, then our ways of thinking about time need changing . . . what is needed for the solution of the problem may be more original thinking; it may be more experimental knowledge about precognition. Probably both of these activities will be required.'

This brings me to my final point. We must realize that we live in a mysterious world, one which poses problems which no thoughtful person should ignore. Mr Priestley says in *Over the Long High Wall*: 'If there is one thing I am certain about, after a long spell of existence in this world, it is that life *is* very complicated, with vistas and depths too often ignored.' Professor Broad stated in a book review in the SPR *Journal*: 'the world is a very odd place and there are very odd people and events in it.' Professor Price said in an article in the *Hibbert Journal* in 1949: 'We know very little about the universe and it may well be a much queerer place than most of us think.'

This, of course, is not new, and such statements in the past have usually been ignored, but new and revolutionary discoveries in science and changing social conditions indicate that the mental climate is now favourable for more adventurous and original thinking on the problems posed by psychical research than it has ever been before, certainly far more than it was at the end of the last century when cast-iron physicalism prevailed in scientific circles. On the basis of the evidence for precognition found in the laboratory and in the field, let us try to expand our horizons.

The cases of ostensible precognition which come to my notice and to that of other writers and researchers must be only a tiny fraction of the number which occur. I shall be glad to hear of experiences of precognition, with supporting evidence if possible, addressed to me at The Society for Psychical Research,

1 Adam and Eve Mews, London, W8. Pseudonyms will be provided in cases in which correspondents do not wish their identity to be revealed.[1]

[1] Since this book went to the printer an important review of *The Challenge of Chance* by Dr John Beloff, the new President of the SPR, has appeared in the March 1974 *Journal* of the Society. Dr Beloff is critical of the concept of synchronicity as it is outlined in the book. He says that 'by querying the concept of randomness and casting doubt upon the classical theory of probability these authors are, in effect, undermining the very basis on which the validity of most experimental parapsychology rests. Nor is it only the experimental data that are threatened by their critique; the spontaneous evidence is likewise called into question. The claim that some real life incident involves ESP rests upon our intuitive judgement that the incident could not have been a mere coincidence. Probability theory cannot be involved in these cases since there is no legitimate way of estimating a probability after the event. If, however, they are right, if fantastic coincidences crop up around us all the time, then our intuitive judgements in this matter are at fault and there is nothing to stop us attributing such cases to chance however far-fetched this may seem from a commonsense point of view.' I must admit that this viewpoint had not occurred to me. Obviously there is not room for adequate discussion of it in a footnote, but I hope to refer to the matter in a future book. Possibly Mr Koestler will do so before then.

Acknowledgements

I wish to thank The Society for Psychical Research, London, for permission to quote extensively from its *Journal* and *Proceedings;* The American Society for Psychical Research and Professor Ian Stevenson for permission to quote from 'Precognitions of Disasters' and his two papers in the ASPR's *Journal* relating to the *Titanic* disaster; The Parapsychology Foundation, Inc., of New York for permission to quote from *Parapsychological Monograph No. 7* by Admiral A. Tanagras; The College of Psychic Studies, London, and Air Marshal Sir Victor Goddard for permission to quote from *Light* the account of his experiences over Drem Airfield; J. B. Priestley, Aldus Books Ltd, London, and Doubleday & Co., Inc., for permission to quote from his book *Man and Time* (Copyright © 1964, Aldus Books, London); Alister Hardy, Robert Harvie, Arthur Koestler A D Peters and Company, London, and Random House, Inc., New York, for permission to quote from *The Challenge of Chance* (Copyright © 1973 by The Religious Experience Research Unit, and Copyright © 1973 by Arthur Koestler); Mrs Jennifer Preston for her kindness in letting me have access to the records of The British Premonitions Bureau; and the various publishers who have given me permission to quote from works still in copyright. I am particularly grateful to Dr Robert H. Thouless for his kindness in providing a preface to this book and for his helpful suggestions after reading the manuscript, and to the American Society for Psychical Research and Professor Stevenson once more, for permission to use the references at the end of his paper 'Precognitions of Disasters' as the basis of my bibliography.

Bibliography

This bibliography is based on the forty-nine references in Professor Ian Stevenson's paper 'Precognition of Disasters' in the *Journal* of The American Society for Psychical Research for April 1970. I am grateful to Professor Stevenson and the American SPR for permission to reproduce the list. It will be obvious that most of the references are to papers in learned journals. Few books on precognition which I can recommend without reservation have been published in the last thirty years. I have followed Dr Stevenson's list of publications with some of my own.

BARKER, J. C. 'Premonitions of the Aberfan Disaster'. *Journal* SPR, Vol. 44, December, 1967, 169–81.

BENDER, H. 'Previsions of Disaster'. In Eileen J. Garrett (Ed.), *Beyond the Five Senses*. New York: J. B. Lippincott Company, 1957.

BROAD, C. D. 'The Notion of Precognition'. In J. Smythies (Ed.), *Science and ESP*. London: Routledge and Kegan Paul, 1967.

CARINGTON, W. 'Experiments on the Paranormal Cognition of Drawings'. *Proc.* SPR, Vol. 46, 1940–41, 34–151; 277–344.

COX, W. E. 'Precognition: An Analysis. I'. *Journal* ASPR, Vol. 50, April, 1956, 47–58.

———. 'Precognition: An Analysis. II'. *Journal* ASPR, Vol. 50, July, 1956, 99–109.

DALE, L. A., WHITE, R., AND MURPHY, G. 'A Selection of Cases from a Recent Survey of Spontaneous ESP Phenomena'. *Journal* ASPR, Vol. 56, January, 1962, 3–47.

DOBBS, H. A. C. 'Time and Extrasensory Perception'. *Proc.* SPR, Vol. 54, 1965, 249–361.

DOMMEYER, F. C. 'Some Ostensibly Precognitive Dreams'. *Journal* ASPR, Vol. 49, July, 1955, 108–17.

EISENBUD, J. 'Precognition, Anxiety and Aggression'. *Journal of Parapsychology*, Vol. 19, June, 1955, 111–14.

———. 'Compound Theories of Precognition'. *Journal* SPR, Vol. 41, September, 1962, 353–5.

GREEN, C. 'Analysis of Spontaneous Cases'. *Proc.* SPR, Vol. 53, 1960, 97–161.

HEYWOOD, R., AND STEVENSON, I. 'The Connections Between Previous Experiences and an Apparently Precognitive Dream'. *Journal* ASPR, Vol. 60, January, 1966, 32–45.

KOOY, J. M. J. Cited by W. H. C. Tenhaeff in *Hellsehen und Telepathie.* (German translation of *Telepathie en Helderziendheid.*) Gütersloh, Germany: C. Bertelsmann Verlag, 1962.

LAMBERT, G. W. 'A Precognitive Dream about a Waterspout'. *Journal* SPR, Vol. 43, March, 1965, 5–10.

LAMON, W. H. *Recollections of Abraham Lincoln, 1847–65.* Chicago: A. C. McClurg and Co., 1895.

LYTTELTON, E. *Some Cases of Prediction.* London: G. Bell and Sons, Ltd, 1937.

MANGAN, G. L. 'Evidence of Displacement in a Precognition Test'. *Journal of Parapsychology,* Vol. 19, March, 1955, 35–44.

MIDDLETON, J. C. 'Correspondence'. *Journal* SPR, Vol. 15, June, 1912, 264–8.

MUNDLE, C. W. K. 'Does the Concept of Precognition Make Sense?' *International Journal of Parapsychology,* Vol. 6, No. 2, 1964, 179–94.

MURPHY, G. 'An Approach to Precognition'. *Journal* ASPR, Vol. 42, January, 1948, 3–14.

MYERS, F. W. H. 'The Subliminal Self'. *Proc.* SPR, Vol. 11, 1895, 334–593.

———. *Human Personality and its Survival of Bodily Death.* London: Longmans, Green and Co., 1903. (2 vols.)

NICOL, J. F. 'Apparent Spontaneous Precognition: A Historical Review'. *International Journal of Parapsychology,* Vol. 3, No. 2, 1961, 26–39.

PAINE, A. B. *Mark Twain: A Biography.* New York: Harper & Brothers, 1912.

PRASAD, J., AND STEVENSON, I. 'A Survey of Spontaneous Psychical Experiences in School Children of Uttar Pradesh, India'. *International Journal of Parapsychology,* Vol. 10, No. 3, 1968, 241–61.

RHINE, J. B. 'Evidence of Precognition in the Covariation of Salience Ratios'. *Journal of Parapsychology,* Vol. 6, June, 1942, 111–43.

RHINE, L. E. 'Frequency of Types of Experience in Spontaneous Precognition'. *Journal of Parapsychology,* Vol. 18, June, 1954, 93–123.

———. 'Precognition and Intervention'. *Journal of Parapsychology,* Vol. 19, March, 1955, 1–34.

ROBERTSON, L. C. 'The Logical and Scientific Implications of

Precognition, Assuming this to be Established Statistically from the Work of Card-Guessing Subjects'. *Journal* SPR, Vol. 39, September, 1957, 134–9.

ROLL, W. G. 'The Problem of Precognition'. *Journal* SPR, Vol. 41, September, 1961, 115–28.

ROYCE, J. 'Pseudo-presentiments'. Part III of 'Report of the Committee on Phantasms and Presentiments'. *Proc.* ASPR, Vol. 1, 1889, 366–92.

RYZL, M. 'Precognition and Intervention'. *Journal of Parapsychology*, Vol. 19, September, 1955, 192–7.

SALTMARSH, H. F. 'Report on Cases of Apparent Precognition'. *Proc.* SPR, Vol. 42, 1934, 49–103.

SANNWALD, G. 'Statistische Untersuchungen an Spontanphänomenen'. *Zeitschrift für Parapsychologie und Grenzgebiete der Psychologie*, Vol. 3, 1959, 59–71.

———. 'Zur Psychologie Paranormaler Spontanphänomene: Motivation, Thematik und Bezugspersonen "okkulter" Erlebnisse'. *Zeitschrift für Parapsychologie und Grenzgebiete der Psychologie*, Vol. 3, 1959, 149–83.

SIDGWICK, E. M. 'On the Evidence for Premonitions'. *Proc.* SPR, Vol. 5, 1888-9, 288–354.

SOAL, S. G., AND BATEMAN, F. *Modern Experiments in Telepathy*. London: Faber and Faber, Ltd., 1954.

STEVENSON, I. 'A Review and Analysis of Paranormal Experiences Connected with the Sinking of the *Titanic*'. *Journal* ASPR, Vol. 54, October, 1960, 153–71.

———. 'An Example Illustrating the Criteria and Characteristics of Precognitive Dreams'. *Journal* ASPR, Vol. 55, July, 1961, 93–103.

———. 'A Postcognitive Dream Illustrating Some Aspects of the Pictographic Process'. *Journal* ASPR, Vol. 57, October, 1963, 182–202.

———. 'Seven More Paranormal Experiences Associated with the Sinking of the *Titanic*'. *Journal* ASPR, Vol. 59, July, 1965, 211–25.

———. 'Telepathic Impressions: A Review and Report of Thirty-Five New Cases'. *Proc.* ASPR, Vol. 29 and University Press of Virginia, Charlottesville, 1970.

———. 'The Substantiality of Spontaneous Cases'. Presidential Address, Eleventh Annual Convention of the Parapsychological Association, Freiburg, Germany, 1968. *Proceedings* of the Parapsychological Association, Vol. 5.

TANAGRAS, A. *Le Destin et la Chance*. English translation published as 'Psychophysical Elements in Parapsychological Traditions'. *Parapsychological Monographs No. 7*. New York: Parapsychology Foundation, 1967.

TENHAEFF, W. H. C. *Hellsehen und Telepathie.* (German translation of *Telepathie en Helderziendheid.*) Gütersloh, Germany: C. Bertelsmann Verlag, 1962.

THOULESS, R. H. 'Experimental Precognition and its Implications'. *Journal* SPR, Vol. 35, March-April, 1950, 201–10.

WEST, D. J. 'Comments on a New Approach to the Study of Paranormal Dreams'. *Journal* SPR, Vol. 39, March, 1958, 181–6.

YOUNG, E. *Forgotten Patriot, Robert Morris.* New York: Macmillan and Co., 1950.

The following books and papers are suggested for additional reading, but this is by no means an exclusive list.

BELOFF, JOHN. 'A note on an ostensibly precognitive dream'. *Journal* SPR, Vol. 47, December, 1973, 217–21.

CHARI, C. T. 'Precognition, probabilities and quantum mechanics'. *Journal* ASPR, Vol. 66, April, 1972, 193–207.[1]

EBON, Martin. *Prophesy in Our time.* New York: New American Library, 1968.

GREENHOUSE, HERBERT B. *Premonitions: A Leap into the Future.* London: Turnstone Press, 1972.[2]

HAYNES, RENEE. *The Hidden Springs.* London: Hutchinson and Co., 1972.

MACKENZIE, ANDREW. *Frontiers of the Unknown.* London: Arthur Barker, 1968. New York: Popular Library, 1970.

ORME, J. E. 'Precognition and Time'. Journal SPR, Vol. 47, June 1964, 351–65.

PRATT, J. G. 'Precognition'. *Journal of Paraphysics* (International) Vol. 6, No. 2, 1972, 44–57.

PRIESTLEY, J. B. *Man and Time.* London: Aldus Books, 1964.

———. *Over the Long High Wall*: London, Heinemann, 1972.

SALTMARSH, H. F. *Foreknowledge.* London: G. Bell and Sons, 1938.

THOMAS, C. DRAYTON. *Precognition and Human Survival.* London: Psychic Press (n.d.).

[1] Mr George Zorab, of The Hague, commenting on Dr Chari's article in the *Journal* of the SPR, for December, 1973, says, 'One gets the somewhat uneasy feeling that not everything has yet been neatly cut and dried in "probabilities", and that we are still a long way from explaining precognition with the assistance of what is known about quantum mechanics.'

[2] Mr Greenhouse's book is devoted to precognition and contains much useful material, but insufficient attention is given, in my opinion, to theoretical aspects of the subject and all too often Mr Greenhouse does not give an adequate indication of the source of his cases.

THOULESS, R. H. *From Anecdote to Experiment in Psychical Research.* London: Routledge and Kegan Paul, 1972.
ULLMAN, KRIPPNER AND VAUGHAN. *Dream Telepathy.* London: Turnstone Press, 1973.
VAUGHAN, ALAN. *Patterns of Prophecy.* London: Turnstone Press, 1974.
WEST, D. J. *Psychical Research Today.* London: Duckworth and Co. Ltd, 1954.

Index